An Old Man Talking to God

The Story of a Journey

by
Emmanuel Williams

My father had a watch that buzzed every thirty minutes. He said it was to remind him of God. I have the impression he could enter prayer mode with the ease of an otter slipping below the surface of the sea. Not long before he died he told me that the whole of the previous day he hadn't been able to feel God's presence. *"There was nothing left but time,"* he said. I could sense how desolate that was. Lying in his nursing home room. Breakfast… emptiness… lunch… emptiness… dinner… emptiness… sleep. How long they must have been, those phases of emptiness, of nothing happening, of nothing to be aware of except awareness itself and the phenomena that enter and exit it, memories, aches and twinges, regrets, loss perhaps. Reaching out again for You and reaching out again and not finding You even though, as he said, he knew You were there.

Who am I talking to? I might say, *I am talking with God.* But this is not a conversation. This is not a dialogue. I don't even feel right about saying, *"I am talking to God,"* because the word "God" isn't who You are. Even "who" is too small. It works for people:
"Who is it?"
"It's Fred Mackelberry."
"Who is it?"
"It's God."

Doesn't sound right. God is only one of the many names we have given You. Allah. Dieu. Gott. Jehovah. Tuhan. Supreme being. Post-its on the sea's surface. Whoever You are, whatever the name, I don't think I'm talking to You, I don't think human beings *can* talk to You, not from here. Not from where I am in this underworld of shopping lists and politics and war. But on the other hand I think human beings *can* talk to You. It's just a different way of talking. Also, I suspect that any and all of the names that we have given to You, our Creator… I think they're all good. I like "Allah". It feels strong and spacious.

If You, Allah, are anywhere, where You are is a long long way from where I am. I'm sitting on a sandy beach, my back against a rock. Late September afternoon. People fishing. Kids are running in and out of the sea screaming. This is my here, my now. Grey pigeons leap on clattering wings from cream-tinted cliffs and hurtle about for a while, then return to their ledges. Five o'clock sunlight irradiates ocean waves, filling them with luminous green when they break. If I try to think of where You are I'm peering into unimaginable distances across unimaginable dimensions. Way out there up there down there in there over there far far far far far away. Also, there is… no *here* is, Godness, Allahness, right here in me, inside the innermost, too close to touch. So close that I feel I can greet You, say *"Hello"*, not hello to the gulls or the cormorants, the seals or the waves, the middle-aged couple walking barefoot along the edge of the surf, not hello to the kids building a sand-castle or to the man casting his lure out into the tide or to the sparkling light of the sun on the waves so bright that I can only glance at it, but "Hello" to the Godness, the Allahness that is within all of this but is also maybe, I think I hope I wonder I guess, hearing me when I turn to You, my Creator, and say "Hello."

I'm finding out that much of the time I'm multitasking. My mind, that is. Even as I ponder the inscrutableness of Your

nature I'm remembering a joke I heard on the radio earlier today… and I'm thinking about an e-mail a friend sent me yesterday… and I'm watching the gray-winged, white-throated gull over there preening its feathers… and I'm thinking about the poetry reading I'm going to tonight, and the poems I'm going to read … and I'm feeling the ache in my back from sitting too long in one position… and I'm enjoying the bright gold light gleaming on everything I look at…
and perceiving that I'm all over the place.

So I withdraw from all these strands just for a few seconds. Separate myself from them, file all the multitasks to be returned to later, and focus without making a big deal of it on this, just this, on turning to You, yes I turn to You, and I am turning to You now
and
everything lifts in me wonderfully, as it always does when I come back to this place.

Down in the crypt under the big cathedral of Canterbury in England there's a carving of a dragon curled around to devour its own tail. It's an image that I've thought about in different contexts across the years. One of the meanings I see in it is paradox. I say something, I make a statement, and either as I'm saying it or immediately afterwards I see that it's not true, but also I see that it *is* true. The statement curls around on itself like the dragon. I was thinking that You are waiting for me to talk to You, to reach out to You, and I think this is true, but at the same time I know that it's not true, because You don't need me to talk to You, you're not waiting for me to talk to you, and I'm quite certain that You won't be disappointed if I don't talk to You. On the other hand I think it's Your will that I seek You, talk to You, ask for Your help, Your guidance, or simply say Hello God. Hallo Allah.

I am able to do this more easily now than I was, say, twenty years ago. Why is this? Why is it easier than it used to be for me to talk to You? Perhaps because I'm closer to death, although I think there's more to it than that. This, after all, has been true since I was born. *"It was my thirtieth year to heaven,"* as Dylan Thomas put it. I think I'm closer to you because I've changed. If I find it easier to talk to You and pray to You and so on it's because I feel closer to You. The gap between me and You has narrowed. So either You moved towards me or I've moved towards You. Since You're everywhere I don't see how You can move either closer to me or away from me, so it must be me who's moved closer to You.

Usually I think of multitasking as horizontal – a bunch of things all more or less equal in importance being attended to or thought about almost simultaneously. But I think there's also vertical multitasking. The black dog over there is doing horizontal multitasking as it sprints across the sliding popping foam after the yellow tennis ball that's rolling about in the surf… it's determined to fetch the ball but simultaneously it's intent on survival, so it's taking care not to get overwhelmed by the next big wave. Also, it's aware in some way of the man in the black track suit with white piping back there on the beach, the man who threw the ball and is waiting for the dog to grab it in its jaws and carry it across the sand to drop it the man's feet and maybe earn a pat or a stroke or even a tidbit. Does the dog feel a loss of canine final self-respect because it has a master? I don't think so. Would I seek, would I welcome, a relationship with You that's a slightly higher-up –the-scale version of dog and master? Yes. Not with 100% ease however; there's a male or maybe human reluctance to agree to a submissive schema. As God is to man so man is to dog. The dog submits to the man, the man submits to God. If I were as close to You as the dog is to the man, then You would be totally at the center of my life. I would be adept at discerning Your mood (if You have moods, which I doubt), at understanding what You want or don't want me to do or not to do. I would learn to obey You. I would spend all afternoon retrieving a soggy tennis ball if that was Your will. I would lie at your feet, one ear cocked for the sound of Your voice. And I'd feel at peace. I am not a dog, however, and neither is God the man who is about to throw the tennis ball. So this is just a way of thinking about something that cannot be thought about. The man would find it impossible to explain to the dog who he, the man, is.

"Here are some truths about the nature of man," he might say, maybe speaking more slowly and loudly than usual, as though hoping this will make a difference. *"I have flown in a rocket to the moon. I have written symphonies and books and billions of text messages…* " and meanwhile the dog keeps picking up the ball with its slimy jaws and dropping it and whining and picking the ball up again, wagging its tail, dancing its small eager dances. I have the feeling that the difference, the distance, between the man and the dog and You and me is very roughly similar, but I could be completely wrong about this. I try to imagine God making a similar speech to me: *"Here are some truths about my nature,"* You might say, in a voice combining a few millennia of thunderstorms with the sweetness of several billion angel-plucked harps, *"I was here before the beginning and I will be here after the end…"* but I'm already totally mind-boggled and wondering when You're going to throw the ball again, or slip a few million bucks into my bank account or initiate some spectacular event that will transform human consciousness and save us from destroying our home and/or civilization. None of which, I suspect, You will do, although You remain as unpredictable as life itself. I think Your way is to give us all we need *including* freedom of choice about how we use all You give us. The rest is up to us. And I don't think You pay much attention to details. You're not concerned about me as an Englishman in his 70s with detachable teeth and an array of chronic minor ailments and financial problems and a wife and a daughter and black and white cat and a fondness for telling riddles.

Multitasking. Back to that Emmanuel. Yes.

Assaulted by an unexpectedly big wave the dog forgets about its owner and the yellow tennis ball, and is urgently paddling the swirl. But most of the time, when not in desperate survival mode, it has an ear cocked – physically or psychically – for the man. Where is he? What's his mood? Is it time for a walk, a stroke, a bowl of food? … all this even as it's trotting down the street or gazing out the pickup window.

"Pretty well all the time, pretty well whatever I'm doing, I remember you…"

The dog's world revolves around the man. Which is how I would like to live as a creature of God. Remembering You as I drive along the freeway, remembering You as I plant cabbages, remembering You as I talk to my wife, remembering You as I watch long Pacific waves roll in and glide across the sand, as I drop my teeth in minty foam and slide into bed. Remembering You all the time, whatever's going on. As the default mode. This is vertical multitasking. There are those who have had an experience of You. Or, if not directly of You, then of radiance that was brighter than the sun even when they closed their eyes, or of a lifting away of anxiety so that there was nothing left to worry about.

Over sixty years ago, I was a treble in a church choir in England. It was Christmas. I was singing a solo in a midnight mass. Back then my father was a Marxist (I was named Karl when I was a baby) and an atheist, but he loved music and me, so he agreed to come to church to hear me sing. Probably tipsy from several glasses of very good brandy, as was his wont at Christmas. He told me later that he had a vision of St. Theresa of Avila floating above the altar, and the church was filled with the perfume of roses. I've wondered what it's like to experience a vision or spectacle that dismantles a view of life you've spent years developing through thinking, talking and reading. Was he sitting there at the back of the church looking at this shimmering presence and muttering urgently to himself, *"This is not happening, this is not possible. I do not believe this…"* even as the chink in his psyche was invaded by a force that melted and suffused him all the way through to the marrow of his bones. *"This isn't possible… this is not…oooohhhhh…."* From then on You were there at the center of his life.

I would like to have had an experience of You. That may sound a little plaintive, the little boy who didn't get the birthday present he wanted. Perhaps there's a little of that. It's not the experience itself I miss having – angelic presences, shimmering Saints, the Virgin Mary talking to me in the back yard, globes of brilliant golden lights dropping out of the sky like meteorites to penetrate my balding pate – but rather the way such an experience surely changes one's life.

Doubts would be forever banished. It's not difficult to doubt the proprietary claims and teachings of a religion, not to be appalled by the bloody fingerprints of sectarian violence all over our history, not to be wearied by the endless theologizing and sermonizing … but a *direct experience…* that's another matter entirely. And it's not just the banishment of doubt, the " *Now I know it to be true that there's a dimension beyond this world, beyond this life we are all familiar with…"* it's not just the understanding that's changed, it's one's nature, or behavior. It would makes one more humble, as in *"I am not the Lord of the universe, or even of my own life… There are domains unimaginably higher than the one I customarily inhabit, where love is as plentiful as the air I breathe…"* And wouldn't there be a kind of spillover effect? If I am filled by Your love, then wouldn't I be moved to love my human brothers and sisters, all of them, or as many as I have the capacity to love and who have not caused such suffering that they are exiled to a place beyond love and forgiveness?

If we are open to them, we are given the experiences that we need and deserve. Is this how it works? Maybe my experience is incremental rather than dramatic. *"Okay, he's cleared away some of his clutter, he's worked at cleaning up his act… let's slip a little spiritual progress into the space he's created."*

I think this is how You've worked on me. Well, fair enough. You know more clearly than I do what I'm ready for. When I compare how I was five years ago to how I am now I can identify clear signs of progress. Clear evidence that I'm not necessarily a higher but certainly a clearer version of myself. How does this happen? You've been at work… or

Your gift of grace or holy spirit has been put to work. I don't think we can turn ourselves into better people. I don't think we can pull ourselves up by our own bootstraps. But I think we are responsible for actions (including thoughts and feelings) that harm ourselves or others and therefore distance ourselves from You, and we can acknowledge this responsibility and do our best to fulfill it by trying not to do those things.

Which can be really hard, God. I think You love us greatly when we're struggling with what whatever it is that we do that separates us from You. You can't do it for us but when I turn to You in defeat and despair and ask You to forgive me and to help me You do. Except that sometimes You don't. So then I ask again and again and again and again and again until the asking is totally true and sincere, or until I've really learnt whatever lesson it is that I needed to learn.

I like talking to You.

The more I write this the more I think about writing this even when I'm not writing it. And the more I think about writing this the more I think about, am aware of, You. That's the purpose of this undertaking, I realize: to remember, to be aware of You no matter what I'm doing. Using my heart and mind to do whatever I have to do to live in this world, to talk and listen to people, to do the grocery shopping, deal with money, work, participate in my community, all that, *and at the same time remember You.*

If I do this simply and in a way that's right for me, like asking that You guide me in all that I do this day, or thanking You for the wild majesty and music of the sea, or asking You to bless my wife Amelia with a joyous heart, or asking You to protect and guide my daughter Davina in her college life, or saying the Lord's prayer or the Islamic zikhir, or just saying God God God , then a tremble of fine energy moves through me like interior laughter and I am closer to the man I would like to be. And to You.

Yes. There it is now. I love it love it love it....

How little I know about You, and how little I know about myself in relation to You, me not as an Englishman with a unique life history (just as each life history is unique) and all the rest of it, but me as Your creation, me as a child of Allah. Is this a recognized life-stage, this turning to You? It doesn't feel particularly "spiritual". It's not accompanied by turning away from the world. I keep looking across the tumbling surf, at the cormorants perched up there on a high rock the peak of which is streaked with guano; at any moment I expect one, two or three of them to spread black wings, dive down towards the sea and hurtle across the wave tops, long black neck stretched out in front of them, wingtips so close to the rollers they look as though they're touching them. And oh my goodness there's a big blue heron up there on the cliff waiting for the ebbing tide to uncover rock pools where it can hunt rock-fish and shrimps.

You ritualize with stillness
stir of wind and water
engrave the random with solemnity.
Through film of clouds and sun you stare
past your own gaunt image
scanning plumes of sand that bloom around your sunken
toes.

I love this world, God. I think of it as Your world. Cormorants embody the Cormorantness of Allah and the heron embodies Your Heronness. The gullness of God. The late–afternoon–sun–behind–gauzy–cloudness of Allah.

This feels more like recognition than revelation. Something I always knew without knowing that I knew it. Remembering/being aware of/opening myself to You gives me a light temperate euphoria. A plateau composed of this feeling is where I wish to live. So anything that reminds me of You is to be happily encouraged. Acknowledging this world as Your creation makes it more probable that it will remind me of You. Whatever aspect of it I am witnessing. *"Check out that sunset! Thank You!"*

I went through a time of great loneliness a while ago.
You may not have been aware of this since I was blaming
my frustrations and failures on You – I had to blame
someone and I didn't think You would mind – so I lost touch
with You, and things I was trying to do weren't working out
and I had no real community, no one I could turn to as a real
friend. I was thinking at the time there's a psychic odor to
loneliness, a dark desolateness in the eyes, a bleakness in the
smile. Members of my species intuitively register these signs
and walk rapidly to the nearest psychic exit. I think there's a
convention – unspoken but real – that if someone is lonely, if
there are no messages on their answer phone when they
return home with the groceries and if their incoming e-mail
messages are sparse then there's something wrong with them.
They're needy or clingy or socially maladroit. I wrote a
poem about this and read it at an open mic. in a café:

Loneliness

It eats at the heart
rodent, sea anemone, parasitic
gnawing, sucking at the innermost

The big dramas, the shock of loss
of deaths and departures
even as you weep you know the tears will cease.
But loneliness goes on and on. It nourishes itself
flourishes on silence, emptiness
like fungi colonizing an abandoned house

Such a wonder it is to watch my species laugh together
here in the café where I sit by myself
stuck in this place I can't find my way out of

The leaning across a table, the teasing, jokes, the gossip
Arguments, mock arguments, the gathering close
For hurts needing to be told, for joys it is a joy to speak.

In this solitary place
the walls hear nobody but me.
The words, sounds, songs I utter
return to the silence they arose from
and deepen it. There is the sense of being sucked towards
an unfathomable hole.

Put on a symphony, talk to God
Make a list, be busy, yes here I am being busy.
Anything to fill the long, the enormously long days
in which I am the only human being there is to talk to
days in which loneliness
keeps eating at my heart.
Afterwards, people applauded, then they stopped
applauding, and that was that. Time for the next poet.
And then, little by little, I became less lonely.
Outwardly nothing had changed. Nobody was phoning me;

hardly anyone was even e-mailing me, and reading Facebook was like hungering for a good meal and being served with M. and Ms. There were walks by the sea, library books, shopping lists, walks by the sea, gardening, marital hugs, increasingly rare poetry teaching sessions in cash-strapped schools, walks by the sea, and long one-after-the-other days with no one to talk to… but I was no longer lonely. There was no identifiable event or experience, no angelic being that I was aware of scouring the fungal desolation of my empty psychic corridor and chambers. And no members of The League Of Citizens Concerned About Emmanuel came knocking on my door to whisk me away for a night on the town or a couple of hours of repartee and laughter in the closest Starbucks.
It was You.
I'm not lonely any more.
I thank You.

I don't know how it happened. Was it because of a change in here? Must have been. I was feeling really bad. The only time I talked to You back then was when I asked You to end my life here and take me back to You, a request that I made on a number of occasions, one that You consistently denied. So I said, *"All right then… if, as seems to be the case, it's Your will that I continue to live here, in this body, and world, then I'd be very grateful if You'd help make my stay here a little less bleak and, frankly, a little more enjoyable."*
Seemed reasonable.

There came the slow getting-betterness of it, a gradual lightening that I don't believe I could have brought about, although I may have initiated it when I asked You for help. It was so subtle that I only realized it had been taking place when I looked back at how I had been a month or so earlier and compared my state now with how it was back then. Very glad not to be there anymore thank you very much. That's quite enough of that.

I would like to understand what's going on. If I understand more clearly what's going on then I will be able to - not that I expect the loneliness to return, but just in case it does - deal with it so that I'm not pulled back down so deeply for so long. On the other hand I don't think You like conclusions. Not that You have likes and dislikes… what am I after here? You never stop. You are movement. The universes are all in a state of constant change. Conclusions, even understandings perhaps, are statements of the past. They're static. Ossification starts here. When we create, when we explore, when we seek to discover and express what is fresh, then we are closer to You. Is this true?

So, no conclusions - to return to the loneliness theme - but here's a couple of understandings both of which are relative to my state of being and capacity *at the present time*.

Right now I'm not feeling lonely and this is because I'm talking to You. The more I talk to You, or, to put it more broadly, the more I am open to You, in touch with You, the more aware I am of You… not You as my creator or source or destination or the You indicated and obscured by the ninety-nine names, but YOU… then the more I know that You love me. If Your love is like the wide blue ocean before me that is always there then I am able to contain a cupful of it. Or a tablespoonful perhaps. I found this out because I had been so lonely. If I hadn't been so lonely I wouldn't have been so desperate and if I hadn't been so desperate... So, in case I forget;
Thank you, Allah for the loneliness.

I don't believe there's any other sure way to alleviate this loneliness. I think it's been there all my life, or at least after I ceased to be a child. I tried many different ways to fill it without knowing this was what I was trying to do. It might be more accurate to say, "emptiness" rather than "loneliness". It opened up in me when I was a teenager. I had no idea what it was. I just knew that most of the time I felt pretty bad, and that romantic erotic relationships with girls made me feel better. Except that they never lasted of course. The members of my species have given me much but no one could love me as richly and unconditionally and completely reliably as You do. In this deeper, less personal way.

Members of my species cannot and probably should not be relied on. Well, maybe I need to ponder on this a little more. Beyond my immediate family there are two people whom I have known for decades and who love me unconditionally. One of them lives in the south of France and the other in Australia so I haven't met with either of them for a long time, but they love me and I love them independently of any contact or exchange. So human beings can love one another deeply lastingly and unconditionally.

Maybe this is a gift from You, the capacity we have to love one another so deeply that it doesn't matter or not whether we see one another, talk to one another, even think of one another. And maybe this is a human scale version of how You love us, as the ripples on a puddle illustrate ocean waves.

If we were living in accordance with Your will I think we would all love one another as deeply as this all the time. If we loved one another as You love us we would be living in a world in which killing one another in Your name or in anyone's name, for any reason, wouldn't be something we could even think about.

How could it ever become real, a world in which we all love one another as You would have us do? My loneliness carried me to such despair and desperation I had no alternative but to reach out to You. There was nowhere else to go, no other source of love I could rely on. And although loneliness and emptiness have long been part of my life, I didn't turn to You before because either because I discovered a solution (which turned out to be temporary even though I didn't know this at the time) or because You weren't yet real enough for me to be able to turn to You and trust You. I didn't know You were hearing me, and I didn't know that all I had to do was quiet myself and turn to You.

I understand that my understanding is very limited. I understand why that teenager keeps sprinting into the sea, flinging down his boogie board and skimming it across the waves. I understand the challenge of it, the exhilaration of it, the knowing you're getting better and better at it. I understand that there's a similarity between this and the ravens I saw the other day twirling and spinning, even spiraling upside down on the strong winds that blow across the sea then come roaring up the high cliff face. I understand that You limit my understanding to what I'm ready for. If there's something I don't understand it's either because I haven't studied it (if it's a worldly thing) or because I don't yet have the capacity, because I'm spiritually unready. I know people who understand a lot more spiritually than me. Most of them are much younger than me, which is humbling. They see and know the reality of aspects that no one taught them about or showed them, understandings that have something new about them, and unexpected, a *"Where did that come from?"* quality. I think those who discover or receive understandings of this nature have higher levels of conscious being than, well, the average. Understanding of a spiritual kind seem to be dispensed on a need or ready to know basis. It could be that with greater understanding comes greater power, and if a person gains great power but lacks the capacity to use this power for the good of mankind then this person may become a powerfully destructive presence. Like Hitler. So I wish I had more understanding. I wish I understood more about death. I wish I knew where I was before I was born. I wish I knew how I could be guided in every thought word and deed by You, so that I would be a source of light and love in the world. But I also know that if I become impatient and try to speed things up I will slow things down. I'll get in the way. I'll obstruct my own journey.

Sometimes I think that everything I do – and I include in this action and speech and thinking – either moves me closer to You or away from You. I lived through several decades of not really being aware of You as a presence within me and all around me. I didn't know that I could, and so I often did, darken my inner. I think it's my inner through which I talk to You and through which You guide me. I was enmeshed in my feelings and impulses as a fish is enmeshed by the sea, following this current, that tide, at home and yet from a wider point of view, in prison, if prison is understood as a place or state in which one has little or no real freedom of choice. Then I began to wake up. It took a long long time. I looked back at my behavior - mercifully without getting too heavy about it - and wrote this poem:

Wrongdoings

I already know about most of the things I did that were wrong.
To be sure there are things I have forgotten that I did that were wrong
and other things that I did that I didn't know were wrong when I did them
and other things that I did that I still don't know were wrong.

And I've already asked God on a number of occasions
to forgive me for the things that I did that I knew were wrong
and for the things that I did that I didn't know were wrong
and for the things that I did that I STILL don't know were wrong.

Over the years I've made a number of lists of the things that I did that were wrong.
They're always quite lengthy.
I'd like to be able to say that they're getting shorter as time passes, but they're not.
Maybe my standards are higher than they were.
I still do a lot of the things I used to do
but now I'm aware that they're wrong, whereas before I wasn't
or, if I was, it didn't bother me as much.
This makes it a lot harder to be me than it used to be.
I've lost most of my innocence about, and my tolerance of, my wrongdoings
but I still do them.
Which can lead to guilt and despair.
both of which, of course are wrongdoings.

I have the impression that God understands this whole business
-the wrongdoings, the impulses that lead to the wrongdoings
the awareness of the wrongdoings
and the regrets, the guilt, the despair
generated by the wrongdoings -
a lot more clearly and deeply than I do.
So currently I'm working on turning the whole package over to God.
Leave the whole issue of judgment and forgiveness to God
I tell myself. I'm still not doing terribly well in this endeavor
but I am managing to avoid judging my lack of success
at surrendering this whole issue of wrongdoings to God
as, in itself, a wrongdoing.
and this, I believe
is clear evidence of progress.

YES!

Were You there all the time waiting for me? Are You there in each of us, regardless of faith, immanent, potentially immediate? I eagerly - and patiently of course - await Your response to this question. Does each one of us need to be drawn into the place of emptiness to become aware of you or to be forced to turn to you? ? Probably not. There are those who were closer to You from their beginning. Why? I don't know. They were born that way. Maybe when they were conceived their parents were in a good state. Maybe they were never oppressed by emptiness so they have never had to seek ways to fill it.

I can often sense, when I meet members of my species, who is close to You and who is not. Not that the former are necessarily higher, or better, or more involved, then the latter, just more strongly themselves. As I come closer to You – slowly, little by little, reminding myself to be patient – I come closer to a sense of who I am. My sense of who I am deepens and clarifies.

Look at me for a moment, God. I'm 72 years old. This is nothing –one million trillionth of an eyeblink in Your terms of course - but down here in this domain it's considered a reasonably lengthy span in the mortal coil department… 72 and I feel as though I'm just starting. I do regret not reaching this place, or stage, a lot earlier. Say 40, 50 years ago. Because by now I'd be so close to You I'd be emanating You-ness with every gesture, transforming everyone I meet with my smile, or sing/speaking wonderpoems to enraptured audiences and changing the world for the better. And maybe I wouldn't have had to endure such an intensity of loneliness. Pity about that. Never mind. It's what the poet Anne Sexton called, *"The awful rowing towards God."* Or, as another poet, Edith Sitwell, said, *"Oh I leap up to my God/who pulls me down?"* No regrets about then, but rather gratitude for this and for now. That's the name of the game.

I've been walking where the sand is wet from the last wave, wet and shiny sleek, briefly fringed by white foam that slides forward and stops and slides back to the next wave, brilliant in the late afternoon sunlight. When I look along the beach I see against the darker headland drifting swathes of very fine pale spray, so fine I only know that it is enveloping me, that I am walking through it, because I see it ahead of me and because, when I lick my lips, I taste salt. This is not an analogy, nor is it intended to be a symbol. It's simply part of this glorious afternoon which also features long high waves, lots of damp dogs, surfers, long-winged seagulls, young women in bikinis (my dragon!) and You. When a wave recedes across the sloping sand I can see the next wave reflected in it. And when a sanderling or a gull crosses the film of seawater sliding across the sand it is accompanied by its reflection and by its shadow. Such details carry no emotional or narrative charge. They're simple. I consider them and witness them and still remember You. There is such manifoldness, such richness and complexity in this world, such infinitely complex interconnectedness, it leads me to think of You as The Great Source of Extravagant

Delight. I am, in a sense, a co-creator. This morning I was up
on a high headland and four gulls floated on a long curving
trajectory from way out there to lift over my head and sweep
around the headlands and out of sight and I heard each gull
as an instrument in a string quartet, rising, falling, sometimes
leading, sometimes following. A lyrical slow movement.
Reminded me of the Wallace Stevens lines:

> *She was the single artificer of the world*
> *In which she sang. And when she sang, the sea,*
> *Whatever self it had, became the self*
> *That was her song, for she was the maker.*

We use the minds You gave us to pump oil from the
planet You gave us, and we use the oil You gave us to make
plastic using the process and machines designed by the
minds You gave us and now huge areas of this sparkling
foaming luminous ocean are clogged with billions of pieces
of this plastic, and Your fish, the fish of Allah, eat it and die,
as do the birds, Your birds, of the sea, the birds of Allah,
and the whistling mammals beloved by Allah. We have
created a very serious problem, one that I don't believe You
will help us with. To The Great Source of Extravagant
Delight the death of most if not all the members of the
human species on this planet… well I can't see You losing
any sleep over it. As it were. You have given us all we
needed and need. Minds, awareness, consciousness, the
capacity to predict the consequences of our actions and

decide whether or not to commit to them. I don't think You want us to suffer, but I don't think You're going to interfere and rescue us from the consequences of our own wrongful actions. You've created a universe, or a universe of universes, and there are certain laws that are probably immutable. One of them, I believe, applies no matter what the planet is like, where it is, how big it is, what life forms or entities inhabit it. It's pretty simple, pretty basic. It says that there are high actions and there are low actions, and that higher actions lead to higher consequences or results and lower actions lead to lower consequences or results.

How can we know what's higher, what's lower? We have grown so clever at interpreting this law according to our own sense of rightness or righteousness, or our own self-interest that it's hard for us to agree on what's right, or high, and what's wrong, or low, although I suspect that beneath all the shouting and the ideologies we all know what we want for the world and for our children. Ideally we should be able to turn to You and ask for guidance, and if we can surrender everything and receive, humbly and quietly, what is Your will for us then we will come to a common understanding. We can, however, and often do, claim to be following Your will, to be acting in Your name, when we kill one another, when we massacre eager innocent children. Can this be true, God? No. NO.

A girl is walking home from school with her friends. There's a man who is certain that it is against Your will for females to be educated, and he steps out from an alley and throws acid in their faces. In Your name.

In your name.

No, this is not Your will, this cannot be Your will. I want to understand this, I want to understand how this happens. How can a man who claims to love You blind and disfigure innocent girls simply because they attend school? If it is Your will that we, each and every one us, seek to learn more, to know more, to understand more, to acquire new skills so that we may be more useful in the world – as I believe it is – then surely girls who go to school are doing Your will. So where does it come from, the hatred that moves him out of the shadows, that lifts and aims and tosses the acid? If this man loves You then he feels that You love him. I think that's how it works. And if he loves You and is loved by You than he knows, not just as a concept or a teaching he heard from a preacher or read somewhere… he knows with his heart and mind and body and soul, that You love everyone, not just those he thinks are right. God loves us all. Allah loves us all. If the man felt this as directly and powerfully as for example I feel this hot sun and cool sea wind on my skin, it would not be possible for him to intentionally harm any of his fellow humans. Perhaps it brings humility to him, Your love. And compassion. Perhaps he understands that only You can know what is true, so it is wrong for him or for anyone to assert his or her belief as the truth and to harm those who may be acting in ways contrary to this belief.

If I were to encounter this man standing in the shadows with a container of acid, waiting for girls to come walking down the street on their way home from school, and if I were able to speak his language or he mine, what would I say? I shake my head sadly as I think of it. An angry man who's sure he's right is not about to listen to me. If I say, *"Only God knows what is true,"* he'd probably reply, *"This truth I believe comes from God."* End of conversation. But it isn't Your will is it Allah? It is Your will that we live in harmony with one another. Does he believe that You will bless him for what he is about to do? Maybe he does. How can I be so certain that he's mistaken? Partly because I see no possibility of anything positive resulting from this act. Low actions have low consequences. The outcome is the blinding and disfiguring of girls probably for the rest of their lives… wounds that persist even after physical healing, like mouths that scream with pain and loss. Screams that echo through the community for a long time and that circle the globe like that Boeing roaring overhead, screams that we hear wherever we are if we still ourselves and listen. I believe that when he tosses the acid the man steps into a spiritual wasteland, a state inhabited by those who are inspired by anger and hatred to commit destructive acts which they claim to be according to Your will.

If I were there watching that man, knowing what he was about to do… if I were there and I had a gun I might shoot him. Shoot him in the arm or leg. *"Bismillah…,"* I would whisper. *"In the name of Almighty God…"*

It is huge, this freedom that You give us. Huge and terrible, the freedom of choice You give us. You know, presumably, what he is about to do. You are aware of the suffering it will cause. Probably he's not going to take any notice if You send him a message saying, *"This is not my will,"* or words to that effect. Can we hear You when we are possessed by anger and hatred? I suspect not. But You could send him a heart attack, or initiate an earthquake, or a bolt of lightning… or You could inspire and guide someone – one of the man's friends, perhaps, someone he trusts - to see what he's about to do and persuade him not to do it. And perhaps You or your angels or prophets or saints are doing this all the time. Locating someone open to the guidance from a higher source and inspiring him or her to take positive preventative action of some kind.

"Freedom of choice" I called it. But are we truly free to make choices when we are filled with anger or hatred or greed or lust? No. And are there other men like him, comrades waiting behind walls or trees with containers of acid in their hands? Do they have a covenant of some kind, a blood oath they all swear to, that they will throw acid in girls' faces as an expression of their belief that it is an evil thing for girls to go to school? Presumably. Which means that the man in the alley is less free to choose. He's part of a team, member of a community, a collective momentum. He hears their voices in his ear, sees their faces, feels that passion. He is a warrior. He will not let them down.

Is an act of savage cruelty made more evil when its perpetrator claims it is carried out according to Your will? Perhaps it doesn't matter. It matters not to the screaming girls with their hands over their faces.

How do I know about this man, or of men like him? I read about it somewhere. Why does this story trouble me so much? Maybe because I'm a teacher. This is the talent You gave me, God, and teaching is what I have done all my adult life. I've met, known, hugged, challenged, laughed with and loved thousands of children and young people. I believe that in their innocence and vulnerability and deep desire to learn and grow children are much loved by You. I think I can say without irreverence and disrespect that we have this in common, You and I. So I know about the men throwing acid in girls' faces, and I know about the mines placed on the surface of the earth so that children step on them and lose their legs or their life, and I know that many children are taken into the sex trade to be used and used and used until they are used up and discarded, God.

It is a cold gray day. The wind feels like a winter message. My right shoulder is hurting. The waves are gray-green. Cormorants are flying back and forth across the ocean like black arrows that forgot their targets. I remember lines from one of my poems:

*She said she knew too much about the world
and not enough to do anything about it.*

I think all of us have always been connected to one another, all across the world. Somehow we've always been affected by the joys and suffering of our brothers and sisters beyond the horizon. But now our human community is electronic as well as spiritual and we know the facts and statistics of the ways in which we help each other and the ways in which we hurt or destroy one another. Thinking of the man in the alley waiting with a container of acid hurts my heart, and causes anger to rise in me. Knowing that many of our children are suffering hurts my heart and causes anger to rise in me. I shiver and pull my blanket up over my shoulders and gaze out across the sea. Is it better not to know? Too late for that. What do I do with this knowing, with what I know? Old man with a minor poetic talent, old man with a stent in his neck and pain in his right shoulder. I can't just give it to You, I can't just say, *"Please take this from me so that my heart may be lightened."* Perhaps I can. Certainly I can pray for them, for the innocent girls walking home from school. *"Please protect them and bring them safely home. And those who have been attacked, please heal them, Allah, please ease their suffering and heal them. And if there is something I can do to help, please show me."*

Years ago I went to live in Jakarta, capital of Indonesia. After a couple of weeks I took a bus into the city to visit a friend, got off at the wrong stop and walked along a railway line. There was a slum settlement on either side of the railway. I had never seen such poverty. Babies lying on rags with flies crawling in and out of theirs ears and nostrils. The place stank of piss and shit. There were people staring into space or wherever it was; they seemed to have sunk into a stupor of despair. I walked and walked and then turned around and walked all the way back to the main road and caught a bus home. It changed me, that walk. I had known there was such a thing as poverty and I'd had my own version of difficult times when I was out of work, sleeping on couches… but this was a level of wretchedness beyond anything I'd ever imagined.

For almost the first time in my life I turned to You and asked for guidance. I was teaching in an international school:

air-conditioned classrooms, huge gym, floodlit sports field.
The distance between the school and what I'd witnessed hurt.
So I asked You – remember that? – to show me what I could
do to alleviate some of the suffering around me. Eventually I
started an after-school social projects club and we came up
with the idea of organizing Saturday night dances in an open
air gym on the campus – popcorn, soft drinks, live bands and
DJs. Great success. With the proceeds our club brought a
Ping-Pong table for a nearby school for blind Indonesian
boys (they used balls with rice grains inside them!) and
sewing machines for a girls' orphanage. Not far from the
campus there was a hostel for market boys, kids whose
parents living in central Java couldn't feed them and who put
them on a train to Jakarta to fend for themselves. They lived
by helping people carry their shopping to their cars. They
were vulnerable to pedophiles. An American friend had
founded this hostel and bought a van and befriended the boys
and drove them to the hostel every evening to feed them and
give them a place to sleep, and took them back in the
morning. Our school club bought them basic readers and
slates and chalk and – I think – abacuses. And we arranged
for them to come to the school Sunday afternoons to swim in
the huge campus swimming pool.

A long time passed between my railway slum
experience and the school club activities. Three years at
least. I think I needed to get beyond white man's guilt. I
needed more understanding of two very different cultures –
the primarily American expat. culture of the school, and the
local Javanese culture. I had to be clearer and stronger in
myself. I learnt that if I witness suffering, if it crosses my
path and I am moved by it, then the best way for me to
respond to it is to turn to You and say: *"Please show me how
you would have me respond to this suffering, and please
make it possible for me to do so."*

Sometimes in my work as a teacher I asked You what a
particular kid who's acting out or hurting in some way needs
from me. It might be quiet firmness: clear light authority and
boundaries. It might be lots of laughter and play. It might be

lots of love. You know everything and I know very little, so it makes sense to turn to You.

I feel like I've been talking to You all my life. Maybe I have. Maybe now is the first time I've been conscious of doing so.

Back in the 60s, I was a lodger in my school principal's north London apartment. She watched the news on BBC TV every evening. She reacted viscerally to what she saw and heard –tsktsking, shaking her head, sighing, yelling at tyrants and corrupt politicians as though they were naughty students standing in front of her desk. I asked her why she put herself through this ordeal every evening and she said, "*Well, they're my people. I have to know what's happening to them.* " I admired her for this. I thought for a long time that I should limit the amount of information I take in or even cut it off completely. Otherwise I'd have to desensitize myself, not care - about victims of earthquakes or hurricanes or the man in the alley waiting to throw acid in girls' faces. I would have to be able to register catastrophe and suffering without being touched by them. Is this true, God? As I come to life inwardly, I seemed to care more about "my people" around the world. But as my awareness of the suffering of others grows, my ability to actively respond to it diminishes with the waning energies of my body. So I pray. That's pretty well all I can do. Turn to You and pray. Pray that the suffering of the people in this country be eased, and in that country, in that city, in that place. And especially, Allah, send whoever or whatever You have available to protect the children; please, please, please, protect our children.

But I'm not so sure any more about the "too much pain for me to cope with" theory. If it's my heart that responds – or rather reacts – then this may be true. But if it's a deeper part of my being – my inner, or my soul – then well, I don't know. You know my soul's scope, God. Where does it end? Are there limits to what it can tolerate? I think there are three different experiences that can harm the soul: heavy drug taking, promiscuity, and extended periods of savage combat. I've done none of the above - except maybe the second, back in the crazy sixties…. So if my soul is in reasonably good shape, perhaps I need have no fear of being aware of my people's suffering. I may be inwardly strong enough to acknowledge it, to find room for it, to pray for my brothers and sisters, and to tell Allah that I'm willing to do whatever You would have me do in response to it.

Are you ever angry Allah? Some of us used to think of You as the big stern judge up there launching plagues and thunderbolts. Or the father punishing his miscreant children. Since we don't know You, don't know who or what You are, the image we create of You expresses the attitude of our time and tribe rather than the inaccessible, inexpressible truth. I find it hard to imagine You being angry, although, well, I might find it rather wearing watching the beings I created whose every need I arrange to have met and whom I love, continuing to cause one another such suffering and to lay waste to the marvelous home I gave them.

When I was a kid growing up in England there was a terrible war going on. I could see the glow of London burning in the night sky, over 20 miles away. It was like 9/11 every night only much worse and it went on for years. I had terrible nightmares for a long time after it was over. I thought of the war as a huge giant – like Goya's Colossus – and later wrote this poem about it:

The Giant

Mummy was frightened of something
we were in the kitchen eating dinner
and she kept looking up at the ceiling.
I want to protect Mummy

*ever since she was crying when I came home from
school.
The neighbors were there
and Mrs. Armitage said
"It'll be alright"
and I knew Daddy was dead in the war.
It hurt me inside
like the time we ran over the dog only worse
and I felt it in Mummy
Daddy is dead in the war.
I asked God to take me
and bring Daddy back
every night I was praying for that.
My Mummy was frightened
we were eating dinner
she hid me away in the cupboard under the stairs.
It's the war she said.
I thought the war would open the door of the cupboard
and find me there
and take me away like a giant
over his shoulder.
There were noises outside, above
in the sky
and crashes shaking the house.
It was dark in the cupboard.
I thought I must be asleep
having a nightmare.
Please don't take my Mummy
I said to the giant.
In the morning our street was bashed all to bits.
They pulled Mrs. Armitage out.
That's who they said it was anyway.

One day, when I'm big
I'll find out where the giant lives
I'll go on a journey
and I'll knock on the giant's door
and I'll kill him*

There is no cloud-high King Kong striding out of nowhere to pull buildings out of the ground like teeth and crush kids huddled in tunnels. We are the giant. We create him with our arrogance and hatred, our guns and bombs and rockets, and let him loose upon the world. We are the leaders who speak of war and plan for war and conjure images of danger, who speak of enemies and threats, of attack and defense. How strange it is and sad that deep down in all our hearts there endures the dream of a world at peace, a dream that is in accordance with Your will, and yet every day, every hour, every minute even, members of our species are killing one another. Can it be, Allah, that defense makes attack more likely? That spending billions of dollars on weapons and bombs, battleships and armies, all in the name of "defense" creates an energy that makes war more likely?
"I got 8,500 nuclear warheads, 17 aircraft carriers, 338,752 armored vehicles, 5719 armored helicopters and nearly 1,000,000 trained fighters… bring it on!"

Hitler was evil, so the war we waged against him was, I believe, an honorable war, a just war, although the nature of modern warfare, the unleashing of enormous forces that found its ultimate expression in the bombing of Hiroshima and Nagasaki, means that even a just war is accompanied by the unjust deaths of hundreds of thousands of innocent people and the destruction of cities. I remember the visions that arose in me when I was a teenager, visions of a better world, an innocent idealism that coincided with acne and sexual desire, and the growing anger at the difference between my glimpses of what is possible and how things actually are. Naïve? Yes. Unreal? No. And here it is again, God, alive inside me, a long furious yell at the horror and waste of war and the greed-fevered lunacy of financial dealings – the dragon biting its own tail and growing fat on it:

Rant
You who reap without sowing

You who are possessed by the need to possess
You who are controlled by the need to control
You for whom compassion is a character defect
You for whom moderation is an unknown town
30,000 feet below you
You who despise those who obey you
and destroy those who defy you
You who exploit and destroy
ancient tribes and fragile eco-systems
you who jump the cosmic line

Listen to me!

Ours is the planet you are pillaging
Ours are the leaders you bully, buy or bypass.
Fat as lava, you boom behind the bulletins you own
impose the brute momentum of your short-term greed
bleed the peasant in his poisoned fields
and slam the factory gates on anyone who cries
THIS IS NOT HUMAN!
Blind as cancer, loyal as a psychopath
the system you created swells and spreads
draining Gaia with its Hydra suckers

You who think you own it, you are owned.
You who think you are its master are its servant.
You are a victim as we will never be.

Beyond the roar of private jets and cyber-cash
Eve and Adam sniff the toxic wind
And scream

Listen to them!

I remember going back to England after several intense
years in Indonesia and looking up old friends, walking into a
familiar room where heavy music was playing and a joint
was making the rounds, and I thought, *"Why are you still
doing this?"* My old friends, my old buddies… so many

times I'd and wondered how they were, and all I could think of now was this accusatory, even arrogant, question: *"Why are you still doing this?"* Getting stoned, sitting together in that numb remote capsule. The same question arises when I learn of the leaders walking grimly out of another round of talks, of suicide bombers, of IEDs and drones killing innocent women and elders and children…
Why are you still doing this?
It doesn't work.
It's been tried, over and over again. It just doesn't work.
People die. Families are shattered.
Nothing is achieved.
It doesn't work.

I want to burst into the conference rooms and assembly halls and dark back-street rooms, the places where leaders fail to hear one another or refuse to listen, the places when men conspire to throw acid in girls' faces, and yell: *"This doesn't work! This is stupid!"*

I'm sorry, Allah. I know a troubled heart makes it harder for me to talk to You, and this is now the center of my life, this talking to You. So can You tell me what I should do with my anger, God? Can it be that as I – with painful gradualness and much falling back – come closer to You I am more deeply troubled by what I see, as though a brief glimpse of light makes even darker the darkness of the world?

We go on trying. That's what I love about my people. So many give their lives, their hearts, their skills and energies to doing what they can to make this world a better place. May they be free of ideology and hatred. May their hearts beat wide and deep and all embracing, like this roaring blue-green sea that stretches out beyond the horizon and all the way around the world, touching every country with foam and music. And please, God, give me a task or a target for my anger. Use me. Use me as You will.

One of my several chronic illnesses is affecting me today other. It took much focused effort to put stuff in the backpack, drive down here, set up the chair by a group of big rocks and then finally sit back to look at the sea for a long time. A hot wire of pain is burning in the back of my right thigh. The sky is full of different shades and shapes of gray. Even the waves seem weary of endlessly rolling in and breaking, sliding across wet sand under a disappearing layer of foam then running back to do it all over again. And there's a cold cold wind blowing.

I remember a time nearly two years ago... It was New Year's Day, and I drove to a distant beach and waited for a long time for the lines to open up, as it were, so that I could talk to You again. One of the joys of being able to talk to You is being able to talk to You, but then not being able to talk to You, which happens, well, quite often, renders one bereft. I say "one" rather than "I" because it seems more accurate. "I" is who I am when I can talk to You. "One" is neutral, relatively featureless, an occupier of space, a wearer of shoes, a name on the credit card – all that's left when You can't be reached, when I can't reach You. It becomes a downward spiral… I can't talk to You because I'm not feeling good, but then I feel worse because I can't talk to You. My attempts to talk to You are like messages torn into fragments, scraps of paper grabbed by the wind and blown back in my face.

So, one took oneself to a distant beach and built a driftwood fire and sat by it for a long time, looking at the sea, looking at the fire, listening to the roar of the waves, the crackling of burning driftwood, and one began to feel a little better… one began to retrieve "I". What happened was that You were letting me know in a way that I still can't clearly account for or articulate that I could choose to go on living or not. I understood that in that place at that time – a North California beach in the early afternoon of the first day of… what was it?… 2009, I could choose to die. Or, as I thought of it at the time, to leave. Which felt quite different to hurling myself off a high building or taking a large number of pills or whatever… it would be a gentle, loving procedure, one that I have no fear of. I wanted to ask You what was Your will about this issue but I was led to understand that this was my decision and that You were fine with whatever I decided, but that I should understand that I still had a load of stuff (for want of a better word) to get through and leaving would simply delay the process. I walked around a bit, gathered more driftwood, built up the fire, and elected to go on living here. I felt like I'd come back into time, back to the sandy beach, the smell of burning driftwood and drying seaweed, the seals smacking the waves with their flippers and tails. I began to feel more positive about my life. Grateful. And there evolved above the quiet sea the most beautiful sunset I had ever witnessed. It was as though all the colors of the world, all the darker versions of all the colors and the lighter versions and/or possible blends of all the colors that no one has named were present, laid out across the sky-wide screen, slowly emerging, glowing for a while then fading, gradually turning into a reddish or an orange–tinted version.

Sunsets

fluff the orange up a
little will you darling yes that's
it and let's breathe a soupcon of that
rather sulky indigo into those
lavendershadowed cirrus meadows up
there beyond the Boeing
shall we
lovely darling lovely and
how about a nice long streak of that
exquisitely erotic pale
olive ooohhh risque
there below that languidly melting
honeycolored caramelflavored
vanillahaunted latte

Was this a message from You? Was it reminder of beauty, not as a concept or a word, but as an experience? Not even an "experience" because that's such a tired word. The witnessing of natural beauty through one of or more of the senses… a single word meaning all that. Ecstasy, or euphoria? No. How about "entrance"? I was entranced. I looked and looked and looked and looked. Sometimes I heard the colors as notes in a long multilayered chord like an alleluia sung by massed choirs in a Gothic cathedral; each note gradually rising or falling but always in harmony with all the other notes. Oh my goodness, makes me tingle to think of it. Tinglehum in the bloodspring. Everything in the universe says, "Yes". It's a yes to which there is no opposite, no "no".

Yeses

Yeses are rising around me
in radiant waves
up here where the headland
slopes to the edge of itself
and falls into roaring and froth.
I'm walking through yeses of salt in the air
among thousands and thousands of flowers
through yeses of yellow
of poppyfied orange

lupinate blue.

Yeses around me are rising
like spray
they open the innermost
declench the knots
tremble and break into laughter.

All around me yeses arise
flowers in ecstasy
ravens are playing and
bright is the light of the sun
on the sea
bright in my face
and the yeses are rising
in me

It was continually changing, that sunset. Just as this sky is today, an extravagantly rich assortment of grays again, like yesterday, dove grays and mushroom, tufts and textures of foam, candy floss, marble-mottled, imperceptibly grooved by silver Boeings. If I lie on my back and look up I see that the clouds are moving very slowly from south to north, as is the soft wind ruffling my hair and stroking my face. I feel as though the clouds are still and I am moving, or rather I am not sure which of us is moving and which is still. What was that TS Eliot line?

Slow rotation suggesting permanence

Then I remember that this planet on whose surface I am lying is turning, even though I can't know this through my senses.

Even in the middle of that thick rock out there, endlessly thumped and worn by the waves, even right deep in the middle of it there's the dance of molecules. There's no stillness anywhere. Or so it seems to me.

You are movement, God. You are energy. There is no profound stillness to be discovered, no ultimate silence. You are movement and You are forever moving forward. It's not looking back that can save us from history, it's You.

Way out there lie the Farallones. Some days they're clear, a solidly articulated form rising from the horizon. Other days they're hard to see, vague shape muffled by haze or mist. Often they're completely hidden, and if I didn't know they were there I wouldn't know they were there. Sixty years or so ago I'd be fishing off the Kentish coast, and on some days I could see France twenty odd miles across the sea, white cliffs above the blue, and once I saw a flash of light which I believed was sunlight on the windscreen of a French car turning a corner. Later I crossed over to France on a ferry-boat and looked back across the waves at the white cliffs of my country, the wake of our journey unraveling in the tide. I stayed over there for two years, so that I was even dreaming in French. By the time I came back You were no longer an Anglo-Saxon God living in medieval churches sung or spoken to in a language resonant with *thees* and *thous*. You'd lost some of Your cultural, or tribal identity. A change that, looking back, I heartily applaud.

When I was in my early twenties I wrote a poem which began:

> *Yeah verily God*
> *you are asserting yourself*
> *too much*
> *into my life.*
>
> *Let me be content*
> *with a couple of beers*
> *a reasonable wardrobe*

and reasonable sex.

The terrible temptation of the soul
tugs at those for whom
the simple joys of simple flesh
are not enough.

That was half a century ago… yes, I know, an eyeblink in Your eternal territory. I never quite managed to forget You. There were certainly unGod phases, but I never moved far enough away from You to be completely free of You. On the other hand I never came close enough to You to feel Your love for me there, always there, in default mode, always undeniably unambiguously there, here, no matter what I'm doing, how I'm feeling, no matter what's going on. If I had one wish to be granted, one prayer to be fulfilled, it would be this – to feel Your love for me ALL THE TIME.

What difference would this make? Well, it wouldn't matter what happens. I would accept whatever happens. That's it. I simply accept it. Knowing, feeling Your love would mean that my soul is forever… not happy necessarily…but at peace. And, yes, I'd love myself as richly and unconditionally as I deserve. Do I love myself? Not really. I am my own friend. I care about myself… remember to say, *"Thank you Emmanuel"* after a walk in a redwood forest or over a remote headland overlooking the sea… like here where I am right now, watching out between sentences for the occasional pelican as it slide-glides on outstretched wings along a long ridge of uplifting air created by a rolling wave before it tilts and tumbles into foam and thunder. Or after a really good cup of coffee. *"Thank you Emmanuel."*

But I don't love myself, not really. Perhaps I know too much about myself. *"How can you expect me to love you Emmanuel when you…"* etc. I know my flaws and my failures. And I can't point to anything that I did and say, *"Look at that Manny Baby! Look at what you did! That's fine! That's impressive!"* All those decades of teaching and – yes, here it comes, the familiar phrase–*nothing to show for it.*

Don't let's go there Emmanuel. Or, now that we've gone there, don't let's stay there.

Because - come here come close…shhh   shhhh listen listen to this one buddy boy…

You touched and enlivened the lives of thousands of kids and teenagers.

If you discount all that it's time to re-evaluate your definition, nay, your understanding, of success. How about this one Manny baby…

As a result of your life so far, is the world:
>one–worse off
>
>two–the same
>
>three–better?

Quick, close your eyes, don't think about it, stay away from the analytic/evaluative/grading mode and answer the question.

Open the box
and what do we see?
A great big shiny
number three!

Burst of loud applause. Even the sea's joining in. They love you Manny. Do that slightly bashful surprised smile, bow gracefully, say thank you to Allah, and leave the stage.

What to do, God, when I am low? My guts are hurting and my energy is so way down I can hardly walk up the stairs. This is all my stuff God… I'm sorry to be talking to You about it.

Magic happens when I enter a classroom. Creativity… imagination… wordplay… riddles… laughter… and poetry. Those with cramped wings are free for a while to fly. It is not, in a sense, me. It's what You put inside me, God, this talent, this ability to open cages and set birds briefly free to fly and sing. But this is not what schools consider important, which is precisely why, I believe, such creative play is ten times more important because knowledge and information merely reinforce the world we already have, they seek no other possibilities, show us nothing different, only more of the same, which is basically more of what is destroying us.

What to do when the classroom doors are closed to me, when *"other priorities"* and *"financial constraints"* turn me away? Is this a personal issue? Or should I say, *merely* personal? I suppose so. It's just that I need to know that there's a place for me in this world, God, that there's still a job for me to do, and when the place is hidden and the job is unavailable or not evident then my sense of myself as a useful member of my tribe is diminished, and I'm left wondering what I should be doing now.

If it's all done, that which I was supposed to do, if I have fulfilled the worldly task I came to do, the work of teaching, of guiding children to know themselves more clearly and find out what they can do, then what's left? Sit by the sea and talk to You? `I tell myself the answer is to be found in what's happening, and this is what's happening, this seems to be all that's left. There are and will be others finding their way into classrooms, young men and women with fire in their bellies, fire and passion that crackle up and down the rows of desks. You poets, you dancers, actors, storytellers, painters, jugglers, conjurers, and especially you fresh teachers with fresh visions… don't stop banging on classroom doors. You are needed in there.

Sophomores

*Ten years of
barren classrooms
ranks of standard desks.
Ten years of trying to do
what they expect
of dead reports
recycled spelling tests.*

If there are two big life tasks: working in this world, and preparing ourselves for the next, then it would seem that for me the second is now paramount. Is this true God? It may be that whatever talents You gave me and skills I have developed are no longer… what is it?… relevant? It seems rather sad, the possibility that I have outlived my usefulness. In the traditional life cycle, however, I would probably be dead by now. Most people died before the age of 72. Those who didn't, well, they were often valued as dispensers of wisdom or good stories. The tribe honored its elders, sought their advice in difficult times, their blessings or simply their presence at births, marriages and deaths. This is not a tradition that prevails in your average Californian suburban town, a place possessing neither tradition nor community.

Outliving my usefulness… from a certain point of view this is rather liberating. I look again at what's happening…

not what I want but at reality, at objective circumstances.
Over the past six months, in spite of many attempts to find
work, to have my writing published, and other endeavors I've
earned just over $40. Since I am still alive it's obviously not
yet time for me to be dead. So here I am, Allah. It's been a
great life. I've seen a lot more of the world than most of my
tribe, and I've loved a small towns-worth of kids, and written
a few pretty good poems, even though I say so myself. And
I've had the great good fortune to discover You, here, in the
core and creation of my life. Is it enough, is it Your will, that
I dedicate the rest of my days to talking to You? Plus loving
my wife and daughter, shopping for groceries and cleaning
house, and writing the occasional poem? Because nothing
else seems to work out, and I'm thinking that maybe I should
stop trying to make things work out and become a quietist.

Ah…. lovely word. *"I am a quietest"*.

Trusting it will be okay, financially, that we'll have a
home, and food on the table, and can help Davina through
college. It would be useful to know how long I've got. That's
the unknown factor.
We all live with that mystery. Well, most of us. I
have a friend who knows when he's going to die, but he's an
exceptional fellow. Closer to God than me. Most of us just
keep going as though we're going to live forever. We live
within many circles, and as we grow older we withdraw from
more and more of these circles. It's a process of
simplification, of downsizing. If the sun is shining and the
wind is not too strong and cold off the sea I am happy to be
here in my collapsible chair on this stretch of sand between
headlands watching waves and hearing their loud respiration,
the THUMP! as a big wave hits a rock and explodes, a
blossoming of salty spray briefly white against green sea and
blue sky.

If I know Your will for me then I use my will to carry
it out. That's the way it works. So then it's a matter of
finding out what is Your will for me. Which, currently, I am

not able to do, probably because I'm not sufficiently clear
and clean inwardly. I will not however turn this into an
urgent issue. I don't think You recognize urgency, although
the Angels/spirit guides who –I assume – work as
intermediaries between your infinite and endlessly vibrant
dimension and manifestations may have a sharper, more
down-to-earth sense of priorities.

So anyway I keep asking for guidance on a daily basis
and hoping that I'm following Your will, and not allowing
myself to be immobilized by not knowing. I remember a
poem I wrote about this over thirty years ago.

Johnny and God

Old Ma Cutmore
used to take him food
until her old man told her not to.

You can't just stop
and still expect
a meal in your belly.

Tom Blackwell found him
in the park half-dead
took him home for a bath.

Tom's missus threw a fit
put Johnny in a wheelbarrow
dumped him on the Town Hall steps.

Richest man in Stockpool
people used to say
six months he lost the lot.

God's gone dead on me he says
I can't do anything
unless God tells me to he says.

Did a lot for Stockpool, Johnny did
opened up the park four years ago
built that homeless shelter round behind the gasworks.

That's where he's been since Christmas
Sitting there, just sitting there
Waiting for God
to speak to him again.

Before I began to have a sense of who I am I was lost to the world. There was a whole crowd of characters inside me who took it in turns to jump into the driver's seat and zoom off in this direction or that. Mostly I was closer to who I really am when I was in the classroom with children or teenagers. This is probably because this is what I was supposed to be doing, this was what I was given a talent for, and the rest, in a sense, didn't matter. Talent is a wonderful gift to receive, and it's good to know what it is because it gives a direction and purpose to life. But talent can make things lopsided. It's probably unwise for example to expect a brilliant musician to function as a normal human being. A lot of teachers - me included - are great with kids but find it hard to talk to adults.

Back to the crowd of characters. I began to sense their presence twenty years or so ago. I called them "Squatters".

The squatters

Somewhere in the middle of this motley crowd
there's you.... the one for whom this place
was originally intended. Most of these characters
moved in
when you first took over. Without so much as a
by your leave I might add. Built their own extensions
blocked out windows, added new ones, made drastic
alterations

*in the landscaping, changed the whole FEEL of the
place.
It didn't stop at that let me tell you.
If any of them wanted something
they'd make damn sure they got it. You'd be amazed.
Moods. Dreams. That death wish you've been getting
lately....
it's not you. So don't for goodness sake
give in to it. Clothes. Music. Drugs. You put a stop to
that thank God.
Alcohol. Women. Oh my goodness me yes.
No wonder so many of them were against
your getting married. I still don't understand
quite how you managed that.
Particularly after they made such a mess of your first
one.
The sad thing is
you still don't know they're there. They're clever, yes,
one has to
hand it to them. Subtle. You won't like this, but the fact
is
they manipulate you. ALL THE TIME.   You still think
you have the whole place to yourself. It would be funny
if it weren't all such a shame. I've been here for years
trying to get through to you. Awful job, to be quite
honest.
Sometimes I wish I'd never....
but that's another story.
Lately you've been sitting in the garden with your eyes
closed.
For hours at a time. I think you're listening.
Everybody scuttles off and hides of course
when they see you doing this. Everyone but me that is.
I run around taping messages on doors and windows:
"there's one in here..." "there's one in here...."
And now... today.... at last ....I've managed to get
through to you
to write all this.   Yes my friend, it's true.
Please read this carefully*

when we've finished. And please don't be afraid.
We'll get these layabouts out of here. Promise. I won't leave
until it's done. Actually, I can't.
But that's another story.

They're still there, but as my "I" strengthens they have a harder job sneaking back in through windows or doors left carelessly ajar. I have arrived at two realizations about them, both of which I believe at this time to be true.

The first is that they aren't who I am. When one of them moves in and takes over I find it a lot harder to talk to You. If I am thoroughly immersed or enmeshed or identified with this whatever it is, then, well, how can I put it?… my content is no longer Emmanuel Williams, human being. It's someone or something else.

The second realization/understanding (and I want to step back a moment and acknowledge quite sincerely and not from an impulse to flaunt false modesty or humility that if I have a genuine understanding it comes from You)… the second is this: the squatters are *lower* than Emmanuel Williams, human being. There are higher and lower levels of being, both out there and in here. And I believe there are two big movements in action all the time. One is up and the other down. One is seeking ecstasy, or union with You; the other entropy. The thing is though, since You created everything there can be no place, state or dimension that is beyond Your creation, so I'm not sure if entropy is permanent. Maybe nothing's permanent. Nothing stays in place forever. Except You. Maybe the entropy part is like the foundation of a home, needed to provide a place for everything, and stability, but destined eventually to revert to earth and then to the life of plant, thence to the body of the herbivore, and so on. Is this true? If there's truth in what I say it's partial at best.

If I am conscious, to the extent that I am conscious, then to that extent I am less vulnerable, less liable to be taken over by a squatter.

Being conscious… what does it mean? I don't know.

Come on Emmanuel. What does it mean, to be conscious?
It's when I am most clearly myself.
Good good.
I am aware of what's moving me, motivating me. I can…
Yes?
… I can tell whether this motivating force, this impulse, is higher or lower.
Okay
If it's lower I can decide not to follow it, be influenced by it or act on it. I can *choose.*
And if this impulse, this energy, has really got you in its grip, how do you free yourself?
What's with this dialogue thing?
It just happened. Follow it, okay?
Okay. What was the question?
If this impulse or energy… say it's a lower one or from a lower level, if it's…
Got it.   Right. *Release mechanisms.*
There are two. No, three.

The first is called etcetera therapy. I am caught in a loop, let's say, a pattern, an interior monologue or fantasy powered by anger or anxiety, depression, lust… and it's going round and round, on and on in me, until I wake up to it, see what's happening, and say *"etc."* or *"and so on."* It stops. Then it starts again and I say *"etc."* again and it stops. Then it starts again and again but each time it does it's weaker because I keep nuking it with an etc. Soon I'm laughing at it. That's the moment of release.

The second is called on when etc. therapy isn't strong enough, doesn't work. Deeper urges. Big downers that I've realized I need help with. Might be resentment, depression, or feverish sexual fantasy. When one of these is taking over, saying *"etc."* is like trying to stop a runaway tractor with a leaf. So I turn to You and ask for help. *"Please Allah, please take this force from me. Please free and cleanse me of this lower force…"* over and over and over again.

There was a time when I was desperately struggling with a really heavy energy that was here in my guts, I could feel it in my guts, and I didn't want it but I couldn't free myself of it then I turned to You, prayed to You for help, implored You to take it from me, over and over again… then it was lifted, it was taken away from me, and I was clean and free. I felt so close to You then. The invasive, less-than-human force had closed me off from my own self and from You, but I had just enough strength left to reach out to You for help and You helped me, and as a result I was brought closer to You.

There's a third release mechanism, the "When all else fails" option.
Fasting.
I don't quite understand how or why this works, God. I think it's a way to tell my inner : *"I'm really serious about this."* I learned of it in Indonesia. What I do understand… no, that's not it… my experience is that choosing to go all day without something I enjoy or that I habitually partake of, for the sake of - for example -an improvement in my/our material situation, or harmony in my marriage, or to be cleansed/freed of a lower force or habit, seems to work. Sometimes it takes a series of fasting days – generally one or two days a week –to bring about a change. No food or drink between sunrise and sunset. Making my intention first thing in the morning. Asking You to deepen and strengthen my fast during the day. Talking to You often. Being vigilant over my inner world, and freeing myself of the downward tentacles as they tug at me. What a struggle it is, Allah! Sometimes I wonder how it would have been if I'd resisted or ignored what I once called: *"The terrible temptation of the soul"*. No answer to that of course. I think I'm more fully alive than I would have been if I hadn't embarked on this journey to find You. Because You are changing me, cleansing me, strengthening me, and on the journey, of which here and now is one moment, the sea air thick with chilly fog, the headlands muffled to vague bulk, the gulls appearing and disappearing like half-remembered poems, in this moment I embrace the totality of it, this journey, the wake unraveled by wind and tide, the starting point as unknowable as the destination. Thank You God. Thank You.

Take care not to mythologize yourself.

Yes. Quite. Point taken. Thank you.

When I was a kid growing up in a small English town I was a choir-boy, which meant going to church twice on Sundays and on Thursday evenings for choir practice. I liked singing and listening to the organ, I liked the language of the King James version, and the togetherness of it all, the feeling I got when we all sang or prayed together or sat in collective quiet listening to the sermon or Bible reading. I don't think I was aware or conscious of You at that time, but I think You were part of my life, like the sky and the rustling of the tall poplar tree outside my bedroom window.

One day I was halfway up a shrubby tree in a wood down the road from our house. It was covered with white blossoms, and as I stood there with my feet on a branch and my arms round the trunk, I experienced a kind of quivering intense light all around me, intense and bright but not dazzling. I don't think I was seeing it with my ordinary eyes. I felt it. When I think back to that moment, I rediscover that fine trembling, or vibration, inside me. I'm feeling it now as I write, and I'm certain that this was what I felt back then. I didn't think of this movement as having anything to do with You. You were the subject of the words and music we sang that were written by other people and You were the subject or the hoped-for destination of the prayers we spoke together that were written by someone else, the sermons we listened to that were composed and spoken by someone else. And even if You didn't actually live there You belonged in the medieval church I attended. It was Your home. There was much beauty in the prayers and hymns and Bible passages and songs, and there was real power in organ music, the big pipes booming behind and above where we sat in our choir pews, as though we were sitting in front of a huge cave inhabited by musical dragons. I had the feeling that this beauty and power came from You because so much of it was so good. The music was good, and the language was often richly poetic because it came from You or was inspired by You and much of it was in celebration of You. Similarly, the church with its stained-glass windows, its graceful columns and arches, this too was beautiful. Sometimes I'd sit there during a boring sermon and think of all the people who came here, sat or knelt or stood between these walls for centuries… thousands of people over hundreds of years. And I would wonder how much of what I felt for You was because of what all those other members of my species feel and have felt for You, back through the centuries and all over the world.

At the cinema I watched news-reels of German people cheering Adolf Hitler. Massive parades. The salutes, the enormous crowds roaring for their hero. German bombers throbbing through the night sky, their guts full of death.

So it wasn't just a lot of people submitting together that meant anything. Thousands, hundreds of thousands of people submitted to Hitler… and he sent the bombers over, and ordered the deaths of millions of innocent people. There was something in this I couldn't work out. Big crowds of people believing the same thing, feeling the same thing, didn't mean that what they believed, what they felt, was right or good. I think maybe I wanted something between me and God that was more personal.

How did we begin, God? Are we all descended from the same loins, the same source? I'm English but I've lived half of my life in other countries. Am I English or am I a member of my global species, a citizen of the world? I'm both. If I had to choose between the two I'd be the latter. A child of Adam and Eve, at home wherever I go. It's wider like this. Makes for a wider heart. Christ loved everyone, as far as I understand, including those considered outcasts. Hitler amassed followers by igniting within them intense pride in their own tribe and intense hatred for members of other tribes. Which is closer to Your will? Loving members of my tribe/nation/culture, or loving everyone, the human species? I believe it's the latter. The global we. Can we do both? Do we have the capacity for both? Yes. I love England, love my Englishness, my fellow countrymen and women. But I love the French and the Javanese and Americans, and I'm grateful to have lived in their countries.

Also, I'm a Christian and love the Christian faith and people, but when I was in Java I became a Muslim, took a Muslim name–Mutahar – learnt the prayers, got circumcised, followed (and have done ever since) the holy fast of Ramadhan, and learnt to love the Muslim faith and people. Religion for me is community; worshiping You in the company of my species makes the worship stronger and deeper. You are neither Christian nor Muslim nor Judaic or Buddhist or Hindu. You are neither English nor French nor Javanese nor North American. You are beyond name and nation, religion and race, color and creed. When we kill, hate or even mistrust one another for reasons of race or religion we go against Your will. Of this I am certain. We all share – I believe – a common ancestor, and it is Your will that we all love one another, or that we all acknowledge this as Your will and work towards realizing it, locating obstacles in its way and working to remove them, whether they be in our own hearts or in the heart of our nation.

That fine trembling, that fine pulsing electricity alive within me when I was a boy standing in the blossoming tree… years later I felt it again. It's here in me, alive in me now, whenever I stop and inwardly turn to it. The Subud latihan. I think it's from the domain that the hymns and reading and churches and stained glass windows and Moslem prayers all celebrate and worship. I think it's the gift of Grace. It's what I was looking for.

Here I sit on a cold sunny December day watching waves climb high, tilt and tumble and wondering if that was a whale making that big white splash I saw in the distance, and suddenly there are two quick black shapes up there, anonymous and weird in their speed and silence, then recognized as sleek black fighter jets streaking across the sky, disappearing beyond the headland as the howling roar of their wake rolls around the little bay like Furies seeking their victims. It's as though they have ripped open the silky cloud-hazed sky, slashed it open like black knife blades. Who was flying them? Who commanded this high-speed flight across the Pacific ocean? Who built these instruments of death, paid for them, designed them, tested them? Who wants them, voted for them? If you added up all the costs of those planes, the fuel they use, the training of their pilots, the up keep and maintenance, how many children could this money have lifted out of poverty?

We are mad. We are surely mad. Please God make us sane.

This is, in a worldly, "adult" sense, naïve thinking. I remember Princess Diana's campaign to stop the use of anti–personnel mines because they kept blowing kids up. A government minister, or some authoritarian figure, said to her, *"It's more complicated than that."* And she said something like, *"What's complicated about stopping kids getting killed?* "

I wish the sky would scream when fighter jets or bombers or stealth aircraft or rocket missiles or drones cross it, as though their deadly trajectories seared space so that it screamed in pain, a scream so loud and terrible people cram their hands against their ears and their faces screw up in terror. And I wish the earth would groan when shells and bombs and missiles explode on its surface, and when victims of war – men, women, children – fall and bleed into soil, sand or stone. A groan so loud and so terrible people would cram their hands against their ears, and their faces screw up in terror. As though Mother Earth and Father Sky, prompted by Your will, have agreed to reflect back to us the horror of our killing, as though they are enjoined to amplify our screams of pain and fear when the dogs of war run howling down our streets and smash their way through doors and windows and bite us to death.

Almighty God
Please
grant us Your peace.

Two brothers and their kid sister are building a dam across a creek with stones. A shallow shaky wall across the flow. They run up to the top of the beach, close to where I am sitting, pick up more stones and run back down and toss them on the wall. The little girl's so pleased and proud to be helping. Bigger stones, more stones. The water gushes around and between them. The boys scoop handfuls of damp sand and slap them against the wall. The water washes it away. They bring more sand and dollop it against the dam. One of the boys is rolling a big round stone across the sand; his big brother says, "*Let me!*" and picks it up, runs across to the dam and tosses it on. The creek keeps flowing, twisting around and between stones in its endlessly supple way. A red-tailed hawk floats over on widespread wings, scanning the cliffs for ground squirrels. The little girl carries a white apple-sized stone to the dam and the smaller boy takes it and says *"Good job!"* and she runs over to where her father is sitting on a big rock and gives him a hug then sets off in search of more stones.

I have a question for You, Allah. It has to do with these three kids building a dam, and it has to do with all the other kids all over the world, loved or beaten, spoilt or starved, homeless or living in refugee camps or on their way home from school, gazing out from the SUV at leafy suburban streets… all the kids in the world, God…

Do they have a future?

After a long wait I sense a *"Yes"* here inside. I want to know what kind of future it will be. Whether the planet will still be our home in, say, forty years. By which these children may be parents with kids of their own, living in a world as different from this one now as this world now is from the world I grew up in. I understand that it's not for me to know what their future will be like. I can only trust You, and pray that it may be the best of all possible futures, and the skies above them are never ripped open by the howling roar of killer jets or anything like them. So, they have a future, Allah. Please protect them. These three kids building a dam, and all their millions of brothers and sisters.

And may the darkness I see in the future be mine and mine alone.

An Indonesian man – quite certainly the highest human being I've ever met, spiritually speaking – said *"Harmony is more important than truth."* This has become my favorite saying, one whose wisdom grows ever more profound within me. Endlessly we discuss, argue and fight over what truth is, of life maybe or of a particular issue, but the major truths are, I believe, beyond our understanding. However, whether or not we are willing to do so, we can all recognize when we are in harmony; and, more characteristically, when we are not in harmony. Harmony is easier to recognize than truth. How would it be, God, if we made harmony, the creation of harmony, the preservation of harmony, the strengthening of harmony, the widening and deepening of harmony, more important than truth? Would it require of us that we always be in agreement, that my opinion be the same as my neighbor's? No. But we would discuss, argue even, without threatening the harmony between us. If we witnessed anger we would seek ways to address it, or swipe it into a neutral zone to die of neglect. Is it Your will, Allah, that we live in harmony with one another? I believe it is. It feels true. Harmony engenders peace, love, empathy, courtesy, respect, compassion, cooperation, tolerance and humility.

How can we ever achieve harmony, Allah? How can we live in harmony with one another? Can we bring this about by decision by fiat, by making a rule? No. And how will we ever recognize and acknowledge what is almost invariably the fragmented, subjective nature of what each of us believes to be the "truth"?

I reached out to You because I felt I had nothing, knew nothing, understood nothing. I was stripped down.

Deconstruction

Something happens.
It's not what I hoped would happen
nor even what I thought might happen.
So I'm angry about this thing that's happening.
I blame myself, other people, fate, the government.
I feel like a victim of circumstance.
I pick myself up   I pull myself together   I carry on.

Because of this thing that has happened, something else happens
which is even worse than the first thing that happened.
I get quite depressed about what's happening
partly because I don't see any reason why these things

that are happening should be happening to me
and partly because there doesn't seem to be anything I
can do
to stop these things happening to me.
I meet people and they say, "How's it going?"
and I say "I don't want to talk about it."

And then, would you believe it, something else happens
which is far worse than either of the things that have
already happened.
By this time I'm ready to throw in the towel I can tell
you.
"That's it!" I want to say. "Enough's enough. I give up.
I give in."
All these really bad things happening to me
one after another, getting worse and worse, for
absolutely no reason.
I mean, if I could see why these things are happening it
wouldn't be so bad.
I'd have something to cling on to.
But there's nothing. I mean, I'm not doing anything
wrong
as far as I know. I'm not a bad person. Not consciously
at any rate.
All that's happening is that I'm getting more and more
depressed,
more and more confused, and more and more certain
that I have absolutely no control at all over what's
happening.
It's as though some irresistible force has come in and
taken over.
It's as though God has turned into some kind of
omnipotent joker
with a totally warped, sadistic, malevolent sense of
humor.
"You trying to prove something?" I shout.
"You got some point you're trying to make?"

I keep wondering what's going to happen next.

The presence of You in my life has kept me fully alive. Otherwise I think I would have been content to settle back into an extended psychic cat-nap, dozing a lot, watching TV during the day and reading spy novels. Perhaps I would've found a Scrabble group in a café or become a regular participant in the senior program at the community center. Gently going into that good night. Instead I'm on what feels like the biggest quest of my life, seeking You. This keeps me alive God. It's keeping my heart alive, my being. Which is a stroke of great good fortune. One for which I am very grateful.

Back to the harmony issue, Emmanuel.
Yes. Enough about me.
Except that… what was it ..? there was a thought back there. A connection.
Lay it out as clearly as you can my friend.
Right. Okay. Here goes.

I didn't know I needed You until I was in that place of loneliness and emptiness. It was a kind of crisis. Rock bottom. Similarly, perhaps, we won't know we need You until we reach a collective rock bottom. We won't be able to solve the problems we face as a civilization until we, as a species, are in harmony… or until we all know in our hearts and guts and minds and inners that, without harmony, we are doomed. Our leaders smile for the cameras as they shake hands but each one is determined to impose or defend his or her national or ideological agenda, so there's no harmony, nor even a recognition of the importance of harmony and a determination to struggle towards it.

Is it possible to love our own country and other countries? Yes, because I do. If I can then anyone can. The only difference about me is that I've had the good fortune to live in four countries. I believe every human heart is potentially wide and deep enough to love not only family but community, not only community but nationality, and not only nationality but humanity. But we have to look for the best in the other tribes with whom we share this planet. You can come live in America and see nothing but militaristic arrogance and crass materialism, and therefore miss its vitality and creativity, even – sometimes hard to see – its openness to other cultures and countries.
I wrote an essay about this a while ago which I'll insert here.

Facing the Bull

I was ill-prepared for North California. And it wasn't just North California – it was Arcata, way up there beyond what's called the Redwood Curtain. A rich pot-pourri (as it were) of dopeheads, rednecks, Rainbow Trail hippies, radical feminists, lumberjacks, Vietnam vet survivalists, and eco-activists. I'd just spent 8 years in Java and had grown accustomed to a gentle, smiling style of human intercourse. Prior to that I'd lived in England –self-deprecation, irony and tea. Two old refined civilizations. And suddenly here I was, at the other end of a plane trip, living in California.
I soon understood why Indonesians call Americans "psychic tigers." When Californians spoke it was as though

they were jumping at me, and I had to consciously resist the repeated impulse to duck. It was all head, it seemed. Head, and self. The Javanese have yet to invent the individual. Prod one and twenty quiver. Americans are the world's most individualistic individuals. I sat in Arcata bars with them wincing fastidiously. "Oh my God these people!". A refined, feelings-based mode of human interaction had been abruptly sucked out of my life. I felt bruised, and bereft.

I was studying for my M.A at Humboldt State University. One night after classes I was wandering the campus looking for my car. Up the hill by the tennis courts? No. Behind the gym? No. I'd never felt so lost and alone and was weeping in a subdued English manner. I finally found it and sat in the driver's seat praying for a peaceful heart and waiting for the tears to stop so that I could see to drive. When a bright light shone in my face I thought I was having a spiritual experience, but it was a campus cop with a large flashlight. Alerted by my erratic gait he was checking me for alcohol or drugs. Tearfully, I told him of my plight. "I don't know how to talk to people here." He patted me on the shoulder. "It'll get better sir you'll see."

That night I had the dream. I was in a circle of English and Indonesian friends, arms linked, in the middle of a field. Shimmery gamelan music was playing and we were dancing, closing in and opening out like the petals of a flower, swaying together in intuitive communal harmony. Suddenly the grass burst open and a huge black bull erupted, stamping and grunting, tossing its great black head with its huge horns, rolling its red-hot eyes, testicles swaying like wind-blown coconuts.

The circle exploded and we ran screaming across the field, fleeing the thud of great hooves at our heels, the rank snort of beast-breath. Finally, panting and whimpering, I reached the fence and scrambled over to safety.

I woke up to hear a voice within me say: *"Next time face the bull."*

The following night there we were again, dancing to softly chiming gamelan music. And again the great black bull unzipped the turf with its thick back, rolling its crimson eyes and tossing its head. And again we all ran, screaming, across the grass. Then I remembered the message.

I stopped, turned and strutted back towards the bull. My abs. were concrete, my pecs. encased in steel, my arms hawser- thick. "Come on then!" I growled.

As I advanced the bull shrank. It was still snorting and stamping and bucking its head, but it dwindled as I neared it. I gazed into its crimson eyes. There was nothing but the bull and me. Finally, I stood towering above it, tough as a tractor, and the bull melted back into the soil like a chunk of black ice.

The voice said, *"That's how you must face America."*

That was 25 years or so ago. I earned my Masters, married a Californian woman, and, apart from a seven year stint back in England, have been here ever since. The dream – I think of it as one dream split into two – changed me. I stopped sneering at these barbarous Americans, as many Europeans still do. I learnt how to do the straight-from-the-shoulder style. I simplified my syntax, lowered my literacy level, and damped down my discriminatory impulses. I grew inwardly to accommodate big vistas and visions. I came to appreciate the freedom bestowed by thinner – or non-existent - layers of tradition. I rejoice in the absence of "that's how we've always done things", the refreshing – if less subtle – alternatives to irony.

I miss the dimpled sweetness of the English countryside I grew up in. I miss cottages and cathedrals. I miss the easy closeness I felt with my English friends. But it's good for English people to live over here. It's so *nice* not to be tentative, to be able to respond to a challenge with an unambiguous "Yes!", not: "Oh, well I… I don't know. Interesting. I'll have to think about it."

The reverse applies of course. Go live over there a while, you guys. Meet our equivalent of the bull.

As technology, communications and trade link us all ever more closely together the possibility of global harmony becomes more real. But we have not only to want it, we have to need it, be desperate for it. We have to be faced by a choice between harmony and the descent – whether gradual or apocalyptically rapid – into widespread disintegration and collapse

Is this what might happen, God? You know what we need to do and how we need to change so that we can do it. When my father – a Marxist atheist with brandy on his breath – saw St. Theresa suspended in light above the altar he wasn't seeking a sign from you. Spiritually he may have been in a desperate state but he wasn't desperate about it. I am exceedingly grateful that it happened because it transformed his life for the better, but I don't understand it so I call it a miracle. But I have the feeling however that something made it possible.

It's probably too outrageous to think that if it happened to my father it could happen to our civilization.

How might it happen God? How might we change so that we can change our world? Because I think we have to change within ourselves. All of us, or a great many of us in a great many countries. I hope and pray that this includes millions of young people. It's easier to change when you're younger. You're less stuck in destructive patterns. What would they need, God, if they are to save our future? However they name You, however they worship You, seek your guidance, they need You, I believe.

I have a recurring fantasy of walking onto a stage in an enormous stadium filled with hundreds of thousands of young people from all over the world. I step forward to an array of microphones which are connected to huge loudspeakers and gaze at cameras that are relaying my image on a huge screen behind me and to TV screens all over the world. I hold my hand up and everyone is quiet and waiting. I take a deep breath and ask You to guide me. And then I tell these young people that I'm speaking on behalf of both the older generations – those of their parents and grandparents – and that I'm here to tell them that I'm sorry. I am deeply and

sincerely sorry that we –the middle-aged and the elders –
made such a terrible mess of things. That through our greed
and our fear and our failure to trust one another and work
together we screwed things up, and we ask for forgiveness.
We ask them, the young people , to reach out to one another
across cultures and continents as we never did and, through
befriending one another discover their common humanity
and – please God please God – their shared need for Your
guidance. Because of us the problems they face are enormous
and can only be solved if they agreed to jettison all old
intertribal hatreds and lust for revenge and start with a clean
slate on which is written in big clear letters in as many
linguistic and calligraphic forms as are needed the word

HARMONY

I plead with them to develop a collective
understanding of what is meant by "higher action" and
"lower action", and I tell them that there are trustworthy
elders who can help them with this. Finally (and I'm not
sure about this bit!) I ask them to take over. To use their
collective strength and power to quite simply take over all
positions of authority, whether governmental, political or
organizational, public or private, and, guided by Your will,
correct all the mistakes we made and set our civilization on a
higher course. Basically, save us from ourselves.

Bequest

The world we're passing on to you
my young friends
is not a place I'd choose to be brought into.
I can't find much to say about it
that's encouraging, and I'm not a pessimist by nature.
I'm sorry. I'm truly sorry. I hope
you find the strength and vision
that we lack, that you will bring this
teeming multi-colored family of ours
to peace and dignity, and heal

the sickness we have spread
across our home.

I'd like to say we did our best
but I don't think that any more.
We got greedy, and we didn't really care
who suffered from our greed, or how.
We ignored too many warnings
worshipped too many lesser gods
sucked and soiled the planet
as though tomorrow were just another movie sequel.
And you're the ones
who get to pick the tab up, pay the bill
and walk on down the ruined street.

Then I dissolve into a fizzing column Star Trek style, and am transported back to this beach, here on a cold raw day with rain and cold blustery winds, the gulls flinging about like autumn leaves. Here's a mini-lagoon left on the sand by high long waves… a pool with patches of sea-foam floating about on its surface. Drops of rain are pippling the water. There's something about the combination of wandering atolls of foam and tiny impacts of raindrops making quick shallow rings of ripples that's very subtle and pleasing.

I see several problems with the *"Young people will save us"* scenario:
One: I'm not sure that young people would be any better than the rest of us at jettisoning old fights and hatreds.
Two: I don't see the older people freely relinquishing power, so there would be a struggle, which is likely to threaten the desired state of harmony. However, it may be that change can only come through conflict and destruction.
Three: Most young people have little or no experience in administration, in keeping things running. There are systems, procedures, rules, hierarchies etc. all in place. Perhaps they'd just keep humming along sustained by experienced bureaucrats and officials and reliable software programs.

And there would have to be a carefully picked, fair-minded group of mentors willing to help young people assume responsibility.

Fantasies show us new possibilities, however it impossible they may seem. Did you fantasize or visualize rainbows, God? Did you set in motion the geological or meteorological processes that lead to light passing through a crystal and being transformed into colors, or the way rain and sunlight combine to conjure an arch of colors in space? How about these rainbows, briefly dancing in the spindrift after-veils conjured by wave and wind:

Aura

.Morning sunlight is warming my shoulders.
I'm up here on a cliff-top
Watching long waves sliding over shining sand.
The wind lifts spindrift from somersaulting ridges
It spreads behind them, soft as mists
that dim the distant hills.

Another wave unfolds and there, down there below me
sunlight fills the haze of spray
and gorgeous, sudden, unexpectedly
like light enchanted by a crystal
colors flash and flare
kindling spray with abalone fire.

Cormorant-black, sleek as a seal
a solitary surfer scans the tide.
A big wave lifts, and as he rides it, stooping like a skier
iridescence flares around him
rainbow halos tinting his trajectory.
Delight it is to see him gliding in and out of glory
as though the elements in all their endless play
enfold him in the ambience of grace.

Sometimes, like the surfer
like the sea-bird floating on a thermal

Did You imagine trillions of tiny whiteness is drifting downwards and piling on top of one another in soft cold banks and drifts, whitenesses each one of which is minutely and exquisitely different… and then bring about the cycles of season, the movements of moisture and temperature and air to create snow? Or were you surprised by the first snowfall, as surprised and delighted as I was when I awoke to a bedroom filled with white light and looked out of the window to see snow for the first time, back in England over sixty years ago?

We humans create fantasies of better worlds. We see them in the future and call them utopias. We see them in the past and call them Paradise, or the Golden Age. It seems that there's always a gap between the world we yearn to be living in and the world as it is. Is Your dream world the same as ours, God? Is there harmony between us all, an eagerness to work together and help one another that is so natural, so easy, that not living this way is unthinkable.

Are we lost, God? Are we as a species lost? When I asked You if the children I saw playing on the beach had a future I think You said: *Yes.* Should I then let go of my concern for their future, for our future, and leave it in Your hands?

The fantasy of the GREAT YOUTH TAKEOVER… it's not going to happen is it, Allah? It's not plausible. It's an external change, a revolution. It would be wonderful and I would leap forward to volunteer my services as an elder who has seen quite a lot of the world and who might be useful. But…

Who are you to "but" Emmanuel ? Isn't that where we
always founder, give up? "Sounds wonderful but…" Is this

too much faith, too much unpredictability, too much potential for change for you? Is your "but…" anything more than an expression of your own skepticism?

When there wasn't enough food for everybody there was a biological imperative at play… *"We need food to survive so we're gonna invade your land…"* Some time in the twentieth century we reached a point at which there was enough food to go around and the biological imperative no longer applied. However, individually, politically and nationally we still define ourselves by what or who we are against. When conflict is the pervasive dynamic winning – or at least fighting - becomes an end in itself. Can we as a species find our way beyond this? Can we widen the "we" so that it's no longer defined by "us against them" but by "we're all in this together."

In England in the second world war there was a very strong "We're all in this together" culture. True, it was defined by our hatred of a common enemy, but it was also defined by what we had to face in our daily lives. We looked out for one another. We were kin. These were hard times and we could only survive them if we stuck together. Young as I was I remember this, especially because I could feel this camaraderie fading away with the memories of German bombers in the night sky, and air raid sirens, searchlights, barrage balloons, explosions that seemed to shake the whole world. *"War is a force that gives us meaning "* says the title of a book by Chris Hedges. Soldiers on active duty experience an intensity of comradeship that the rest of us rarely know, if ever. How paradoxical it is that we come closest to one another when we are intent on destroying members of our species.

What does this mean, God? If adversity is a more effective way of bringing us together than any other, will we as a species turn to harmony only if we are threatened with annihilation? Will things get so bad that we turn to You as our last chance? Turn to You whatever our religion, belief or non-belief? There was a reason why You sent my father the experience he had, the vision of St. Theresa poised in the space above the altar. Perhaps someone prayed for him. Perhaps it was the sight and sound of his eldest son singing an anthem in a crowded church. When we witness the effects and don't understand the cause we call it a miracle, but I think there's always a cause, a trigger. How many of us need to pray to You for help before You are moved to help us to save ourselves? Is it to be a matter of a cumulative crescendo of prayer, of hundreds of thousands, even millions of us reaching out and up to You together, asking over and over again for guidance and strength? Or is it to be a collective yell as we confront some awful terrestrial calamity? I have a strange, bleak feeling that individual mortality isn't that important to You, that if we simply carry on oblivious of You then You will simply allow us to plunge over the cliff. This is not our earth, it's Yours.

The Promise

I will always remember
that the world is not mine
that the strength in this body
the thoughts in this mind
the feelings that flow
in and out of this heart
the life that quickens this being
these are not mine.

Such was the promise I made
when the universe burst into life
when paradise rose
in the morning of time
and welcomed my breath
my tentative step.
Nothing is mine
save the vow to remember.

When I forget
when the promise is broken
when the source of all life

I remember when the riots happened in Los Angeles in 1992; there were dozens of deaths and hundreds of buildings torched. A friend with considerable street smarts drove me down Hollywood Boulevard in his big Cherokee Jeep… my family and I were staying with him because his home seemed the safest place to be, especially since I'd been held up at gunpoint and had my car driven away and felt as though a psychic hole had been drilled in me and that I couldn't protect my wife and our newborn baby daughter Davina. As we drove down Hollywood Boulevard we could see people smashing store windows and carrying TVs and computers to their cars, and others setting fire to buildings. He had no fear even though ours was the only vehicle moving on the street. It was very reassuring, although I kept expecting someone to shoot at us. His huge dog was sitting behind me, close enough for me to hear its breathing. Later, in his home, we were doing our Subud latihan and I saw or felt myself standing in the streets in the middle of the chaos. I was growing taller and taller… finally I felt as tall and strong as the Statue of Liberty, and I held my arms out over the city and sang a slow peaceful melody that calmed the feelings of all who heard it. Meanwhile my friend – he told me afterwards – was zooming around the streets with a giant spray can zapping anger and hatred and violence wherever he encountered them. Later, when we sat out on his veranda drinking tea, the atmosphere out there seemed cooler and lighter. The worst was over.

Next day the big cleanup started. I was trying to remember the melody I had been singing when I was standing high over the city, but I couldn't. So then I was trying to think of a song or a piece of music – Greensleeves maybe, or a slow movement from a Mozart piano concerto,

or Samuel Barber's Adagio, something that everyone would be touched by, and I couldn't hear it. Beethoven's Ode to Joy? John Lennon's Imagine? Bach's Air on a G. string? We people living in this enormous city the day after anger blew the lid off Pandora's Box… we all had so much in common as members of the human species, and as hundreds of us worked together to heal our communal wounds and clean up the debris I wanted to call music stations and request music that would touch and lift all feelings as I had sung the previous day in my experience, but we were… how to put it?… divided by our tastes, our musical preferences. Those who like gospel wouldn't like mariachi, those who liked hip-hop wouldn't like classical, and so on. When I was as lofty as the Statue of Liberty what I was singing came from You, or so it seemed when I looked back. When I returned to being just me I couldn't hear the music You passed through me. Was there ever a time when we all loved the same music, when we
all lived together in what might be called the collective heart and not segregated into our minor tribes or subgroups, members of this niche or that, separately situated on "The Long Tail"? Probably not. Or, only in the Golden Age.

How will we ever be able to put together a framework of higher and lower, or finer and coarser, that finds universal, or at least clear majority, agreement? Are You there, God? Maybe as far as You're concerned we already have the guidelines we need. You sent them at various points in our history through a line of messengers or prophets, people whose hearts were clean and whose souls were high so that they could listen to You, receive what You wanted us to be given and passed on without distortion. The "thou shalt nots…" the "woe unto those who…"

There are virtues to help us. Abstract words whose existence point, individually and collectively, to a higher, better, more life-enhancing domain. They endure, not just as words but as, well, presences perhaps, imminences, potentials, reminders, sturdy ropes to clutch, whose capacity to support us is limited only by our capacity to be true to them. Here are some virtues:

Harmony…… Simplicity…… Compassion… Faith…
Fortitude… Sincerity… Integrity…

Such qualities are like the sound of bells in the sky. Like columns of radiant light. I think the quality or virtue each word represents, is a name for, is familiar to us all and recognized by us all even though the name varies according to language. And I think they meld. Practicing one of them brings us to a domain in which the others are closer. I think they are peaks in the enormous range and sweep of your creation. There is the cormorantness of God, and there is the harmoniousness of God. And, yes, I suppose the same is true of the dark low qualities – greed, hypocrisy, lust, cruelty etc. so I suppose there's the cruelness of God. This is hard to contemplate. You have the power to stop the man waiting in the alley with a container of acid but You don't. From a certain perspective this non-action – when all actions are Yours to take – is cruel. And I know, or I think I know, why You allow him to step out into the street and do what he's there to do.

Freedom of choice. Yes. I was talking to You about this before. But this morning I was thinking about freedom of choice again. I was remembering a school I once started and ran for a year way up in North California… A dozen or so seven to nine-year-olds. I gave them freedom of choice. With parent support I created a place where all the materials and equipment they might need were at hand. Garden. Kitchen. Library. Woodwork tools. Paint brushes, paper, easels. Montessori–style math apparatus. Kind of like You creating the world and putting us on it. Anyway, there were children who, after a day or two of checking the place out – and me of course – got down to work with an ease and focus that was wonderful to behold. There were two or three, however, who'd spent time in more conventional schools and who were overwhelmed by this degree of freedom. So I'd give each one of them a choice between, say, two activities:
"Well, you can create a long comic strip story with that roll of paper, called 'The girl who wanted to be a mermaid' or

you could make cubes and paint each side a different color..."

These children weren't ready for wide open freedom. If I hadn't narrowed things down for them they would have been overwhelmed and unhappy. I was following what I once heard described as: "The theory of diminishing crutches." You have a hand on each of the child's shoulders, you've given him a pair of crutches; and you tell him to step in this direction with this foot, then with this foot… and so on. As the child gains skill and confidence you progressively withdraw guidance and support. The teacher makes herself unnecessary, and the child moves towards autonomy.

Our only rule in the school was, *"Don't choose to do something just because someone else is doing it."* We had talked about sheep, about how they tended to follow one another even if it meant jumping over a cliff. So occasionally, rising out of the busy hum, there'd be the sound of children making sheep noises: " *Baaaa baaaa!*" and someone saying, *"I'm not sheeping! I'm not sheeping!"*

Clearly this is not the way You do things. I'm making my way towards another question, Allah. It's one that has often been asked in various forms at various times: *"Why do you give us freedom that we are unable or not ready to handle?"* Which is a re-phrasing of: *"Why do You allow such suffering in the world?"*

I once wrote a story in which a young man was lifted – in his spiritual body – high above the surface of the planet, and left there for a while, poised and motionless in space as the earth slowly turned beneath him. He was hearing what sounded like huge waves of voiced anguish rising, not from oceans or deserts or mountain ranges, but from human communities. When he returned to Earth he was astonished that people seemed okay, driving their cars and SUVs around, dropping off their kids at school, working in the places where people work and watching sports on TV. He thought maybe what he'd heard was from regions where wars were being fought, or from communities devastated by natural catastrophes, and he told himself that this was the truth, even though he suspected that the sound came from pretty well everyone. Because pretty well everyone was spiritually lost, and that this was the reality of life here on earth. Anguish. Lostness. Separation from You.

I think that when we are really lost or when we urgently need a boost You send us a reminder of where we come from and how we should live if we want to go back there to You. Prophets through whom you speak. Messages that become books clarifying how we should live, how we should love and care for one another. I'm thinking we're fast approaching, or have already entered, another time in which we are truly lost. And I'm wondering, if this be true, if and how You will respond, or have responded.

I watched a surfer this morning riding a wave. As he neared the end of his ride he flipped upwards off the back of the wave and executed a perfect somersault, whooping as he did so. It made me laugh out loud to watch him, to witness the sheer mastery of the move. I love my people, God. Your people. Please help us.

I was at a spiritual gathering in California back in the 'eighties. As you know, God, I'm a member of Subud, a gift you sent down to us about eighty years ago. I was on my way to do the Subud spiritual exercise called latihan when a woman I knew vaguely came up to me and told me a heart-rending story about her teenage son, about how he was getting heavily into drinking and drugs, hanging out with kids she didn't like at all. She was crying as she spoke. I gave her a hug and said I'd be very willing to meet with him if he was open to that. Then I went to the latihan in a big room with my Subud brothers, and during it I was seeing crowds of young people, teenagers, down near the bottom of a deep lake. They were trapped down there and were struggling to reach the surface but there were dense layers of weed between them and the surface, and they couldn't get through it. They were struggling with the weed and getting tangled up in it. I could hear them screaming for help as they tried to disentangle themselves. I was feeling their state, feeling it all through me. It was devastating.

Then I was walking along a road and came to a big dark cloud. There were crowds of teenagers lost in the cloud trying to find their way out, and crying out for help. I was stricken by this and ran into town and was knocking on the doors of people's homes, telling everyone there were all these teenagers lost in a huge dense cloud up at the end of the street and they needed help urgently, they needed to be shown how to find their way out of the clouds so that they wouldn't be lost any more. No one was willing or able to help. They were all too busy. Now was not a convenient time. Come back later, could you? Tomorrow maybe. I couldn't do it on my own. It was too much. I felt helpless and desperate.

If we're not inwardly alive, spiritually alive, then, like the people on whose doors I knocked we will have little or no sense of the deeper needs of young people.

My own good

You're taking something from me
that's precious to me and almost unknown.
You're taking me away from who I am
burying me too deeply for me to retrieve myself.

You don't know what you're doing to me
because who you are is no longer alive in you.
You think you're giving me what I need
you think what you're doing is all for my own good.

You don't know any better.
You don't know who I am.
How can you? You don't know who you are.

I don't blame you. I don't know who's to blame.

You're older than me. More powerful.
You've organized the world in such a way
that if I do not do what you expect of me
you tell me that I've failed, and make me feel it.

I make myself believe you. It's easier.
If I question your expectations and requirements
and try to tell you why I question them
you make a 'rebel' of me. That's not the issue.

You control the world. The world
is where I live. And so I tell myself
it's easier to give in to you
play the game according to your rules.

What choices do I have? Sometimes I try to follow
what I want to follow
do what I feel moved to do, according to
my sense of who I am, of what's right for me.

If I don't, I won't know who I am.
And if I don't know who I am
how can I live my life, how can I know
that what I do is me, that this is why I'm here?

Perhaps that's why it all keeps going wrong.
People don't know who they are.
What they believe, what they live by,
comes from somewhere else.

You'll tell me that I'm confused.
You'll tell me that I'm going through a "phase"
that my priorities are wrong.
You'll advise and counsel, threaten, punish.

There may be moments when you smile wryly
and look back through the years

and say, "I used to feel like that
a long long time ago."

And you might wonder when things changed
what was gained and what was lost.
And when you do, perhaps at last
we will be able to talk to one another.

The high-school students I work with as a poet in the schools probably don't know that they may be spiritually lost, although many of them struggle with a sense of emptiness and isolation. I am not allowed to refer to You when I talk with them. Sometimes, however, I tell them a true story: *"When I was living in Indonesia some of us westerners got together and started a pottery enterprise. We built a workshop and kilns and brought materials and equipment and put a young man –David – in charge. Unfortunately the enterprise did not go well, and after a while the business people had a meeting with David in one of their houses. I was downstairs while it was going on. I could hear them giving David a hard time. Then I saw him walk down the stairs, across the hall and out through the front door. Which was strange because I could still hear the businessmen yelling, and David answering them. Later I told him I had seen him leaving but the meeting had continued as though he was still there, and he laughed and said that he guessed he was having such a bad time he left, or his soul left.*

So the word soul could be used for that part of us that's inside and can't be seen. It can go anywhere, take any shape... It might be that part of you that leaves when you're sitting in a classroom feeling bored and you're at home in your room or hanging out with your friends. So try writing a poem entitled, "My soul." Or "My spirit..." or even "The real me..."

Mostly they respond to this and many write strong, deeply-felt poems.

It isn't much, God, not when I think of the teenagers

trying to claw their way through thick tangled weed clumps to reach the light. There's nothing in the high school or college curriculum and little in our contemporary culture that responds to this need, to this emptiness and isolation. Also, I believe we must be psychically clear and conscious if we are to find our way to You, or for You to touch us, touch our souls with Your love. Many teenagers and young people are either locked into their minds as they cope with endless school assignments or they're dimming their consciousness – and therefore their essential humanity - with drugs or binge drinking, or spiritually damaging themselves by sleeping around, or "hooking up." They're rarely, if ever, in a state of simple quiet.

One day I will write what I understand about seeing young people trying to fight their way through thick weeds, or out of the dense dark cloud… I will write about drugs and alcohol and hooking up and how these experiences affect them. I will write as though I were talking to teenagers, openly, non-judgmentally, directly. Then I will seek ways to make this accessible to them so that they read or listen or watch and think for themselves about what I've said, because I sincerely believe they need to think about their souls and You and about what they believe, about how they live.

I would be grateful for any help I'm entitled to from You or from any of the legions of angels or spirit guides out there somewhere. I'll start when I finish this.

Yes.

Wintertime. Early in the new year, huge waves looking clean and pure as tinted fluid glass, bright jade rollers with white crests, rainbows briefly hovering in spindrift. Gravel, seaweed and crab-shells strewn across walkways and the Seaview Motel carpark by the high tide that came roaring in at dawn. Too cold to sit on the beach and talk to You, so I'm here in the back garden, windchimes merrily dingling, fir and eucalyptus trees whispering to one another in the winter sunshine.

Strange to be approaching my life's end and yet feel as though I am really discovering You, sensing You, becoming aware of You for the first time. Or rather, in ways I've never been aware of You before. Which is a beginning. When my father died, inscribed on his gravestone–at his request–was T.S. Eliot's line:

In my end is my beginning.

Things I believe to be true about You include:
You are infinite
You are the creator of all that is
You were there before the beginning and You will be there after the end
You cannot be known or understood or measured or defined by me or indeed by anyone
You endow all that exists and all that lives with the capacity to worship You, including stones, cabbages, lemurs, and mathematicians.
You love Your creation, as wolves and elephants and humans love their children. You love me. You love us all and You love me.

All this I believe to be true, God. The truth is that I would like to know, to experience, to discover with my nose-hairs and my vertebral discs, clean of ego and solemnity, is the last one in the above list. I would like to feel Your love for me.

I do already, Allah, to the extent that I am capable of doing so. It's subtle and pervasive, and if it left me, if it was somehow cut off then I think I would feel like a dying fish in the tide, completely enmeshed by the forces within me and all around me. And I would be maimed and darkened by whatever acts I had perpetrated that caused You to cease loving me, like Macbeth when he discovered that he could no longer pray to You. Please God never let me do anything like that.

I want more of it. That's what I want to tell You. Please

God may I feel more of Your love for me. Even as I say this
to You I know I am immersed in the infinite abundance of
Your love entering me through every pore at every moment,
so I can't really ask You to love me more. Well I can but it's
kind of redundant. I can only ask You to clean and widen and
deepen and open me so that I'm able to feel Your love more
fully. Yes that's it. Please, Allah, if it be Your will, please
make it possible for me to feel Your love for me more fully.

I remember, thirty years or so ago, an experience that
makes me smile now when I think back on it. I was in
Arcata, way up at the top end of California. I was earning my
M.A. in the teaching of writing. I was on my way to a
Saturday evening concert in the University concert Hall. I
think it was classical music. I was walking across the campus
with a group of friends. There was a girl who played the flute
whose name was Squirrel, and a stumpy little guy, a Vietnam
vet with whom I occasionally did poetry readings in a bar
called the Jambalaya. Steve Miller. He used to tell me about
terrible experiences he'd had in the war as a tunnel rat –
crawling into tunnel systems dug by the Vietcong, checking
them for villagers or booby-traps, or the enemy. One day I
wrote a poem about him. Took it to his apartment. He was
sitting in the kitchen with a couple of buddies drinking
coffee and working on a joint. I poured myself some coffee
and said no to the joint. As I read the poem he closed his
eyes and slid slowly off his chair and ended up curled like a
fetus under the kitchen table.

Vet
- for Steve Miller

He's seen too much
he's over-exposed
passed beyond all limits years ago
smashed all the statues he encountered
detonated several hundred minor gods
found the happy medium by accident

and lost it in a bar downtown.

What truths remain intact
which myths still hold
their meaning? Every night
another bomb destroys the kitchen
the street erupts
with screams and burning limbs.

Pray for him my friends.
There's no place left for him to run to
They snarl behind their triggers
dodge the mines
behind his eyes
and close in
for another
final
kill

So there we were on our way to the concert and a
``Humboldt bud'' joint was passing around and it came to
me and, as though I had walked into a time warp, I took a
couple of hits, first time for over 15 years, and minutes later I
couldn't feel You any more. I was cut off from You. I felt
like an astronaut whose connections with the mother-ship
had all been severed. I was lost and adrift in darkness and
emptiness. Basic systems – breathing, circulation etc. -
functioning. The rest of me was in deep funk mode,
existential panic. I left the concert hall and wandered around
the campus. Found a room in the music building and played
piano for a long time, then crouched in a corner whimpering
and saying over and over again, "I'm sorry God… I'm
sorry…" Went to the restroom, drank a lot of water, made
myself vomit. Later Steve found me on a bench trembling.
Put his arm around my shoulders and sat with me for a long
time. Gradually I came back to myself and to You.

Many of the tastes and sounds and surfaces of the
world we've created are harsh and bitter, God. Money stuff
sex stuff anger and violence. It oppresses us even when we're

not aware of being oppressed. This is my understanding, God, incomplete as always and relative to now. The energies in a joint or in cocaine or heroin or alcohol are plant forces. Reactive, alive in a very limited, passive mode, but gentler than the harsh materialistic world we inhabit most of the time, so it feels nice to go there. But we can't be in the plant world and in our human world at the same time. When we go there we lose our human consciousness, our ability to reason, to decide, to relate to those not here with us in the plant domain, and we cut ourselves off from You. Hundreds of thousands, possibly millions of my people are regular visitors to this beguiling forest, and many are lost in there.

Addict

*the now back then not
long ago recent in fact the
now was only when
the need met what was needed and yes o
yes sweet relief there was the rush
the bliss how it feels when
the need is met that was the only now no other bliss
there can be no other bliss
not while the need is needing what it needs*

*there is the need there is the giving to it
what it needs there is the
bliss felt when the need is met is
given what it needs
but the meeting
of fulfillment of the need
this is the only now and soon it fades away it goes
away the bliss dims then the now is
nothing but a waiting for another now
which is not a now at all
the waiting is not a now it is a
meanwhile it is a soon it is not
a now
the need comes back stronger*

each time the need is
stronger more at home each time
and in the now that is the meeting of the need the
bliss is fading the bliss dims
is no longer blissful not as it was
but less the bliss

so then the purpose of the need is simply to
supply itself with what it needs so that it
survives so that it grows so that
it gets bigger and bigger
so that its demands its
particular requirements be met so then eventually sooner or
later the organism
the need is using so that it be fulfilled so that it
may be fed so that it grows
is destroyed
the organism is
des-
troyed
the organism is a human being
one
of
us.

maybe the human being can say
please help me God
or
friends, please help me.
maybe the human being can say
no more
no more
can tell the need you are not me
this is not your home
this is my home
can say this
over and over again
over and over and over again

Biggest waves I've seen for years. When I look out across the ocean beyond them it seems quite placid. No white horses. No fuss or foam. But sixty, seventy yards out they rise seemingly out of nowhere, and the steep rolling walls are streaked and marbled by foam from their predecessors, and they roll forward in a thickly frothy mantle like avalanches tumbling down a mountainside. They make a constant thunderous roar and an occasional THUMP! like a deep bass drum, with an undertone of growling inside it, echo of a enormous sea monster way out there down there deep down there.

Two children, big brother little sister, are standing on the edge of thunder and tumult, scampering across the slip slap sheen of the last wave, scooping handfuls of sand to chuck at the sea as though to drive it back towards the horizon, and suddenly there's a REALLY BIG WAVE hissing at their feet and they're screaming and sprinting up the sloping sand with the REALLY BIG WAVE right behind them, swallowing their footprints, loud and scary as a dragon.

There's another little girl, little sister, over by the rocks, and here's the mother with a toddler baby on her arm and, it would seem, another on the way, and here's the father who takes the toddler baby and set her down on the sand, holding out her arms and singing to her she tries to walk. I close my eyes and listen to the roar, to the screams and yells of the kids. A warm afternoon in winter, just me and the family, sunlight bright red against my closed eyelids. This I want, nothing but this, as it is, the children, the dad with his mustache and sunglasses, mom in her pink PJ bottom-looking slacks, a boy with his soaked blue jeans, "Mexico" printed on the back of his green tee-shirt, and the huge waves unbundling in slow succession… and the rocks over there, and the black cormorants hurtling over white chaos… I'm glad they're here, the Mexican family members. It's not just me on the beach, it's us. We are here on the beach, enjoying the sun's warmth, watching the waves rolling, not really "together" in any meaningful sense, a loose "we", I'd say, but we nevertheless. I'm glad that I feel love for this father and this mother, this son, this tough little girl dancing on the brink of the growling waves and this younger sister, slightly pudgy, not ready to approach the sea without a hand in her mother's hand, and the baby toddler holding one arm out as though greeting everything, and the fetus in there hearing heart beats and voices and resonance of the ocean thunder.

Now you've gone. I see your footprints. I see the sea wall the son built, a hummock smoothed by longer waves. The tide's going out. The sun's going down.

People

Sometimes
as we pass one another in the street
I look at your face, at your eyes
at the way you move
at the way you stand on the sidewalk
waiting for the lights to change
and I feel your life in you.
I feel in a way that I can't explain or describe
who you are
I feel the story of you
the past that is yours to remember
I sense the nature of you
like a glow or a scent
an aura of energy
uniquely and inwardly yours.

I look at you in supermarkets
scanning the cereals
probing at melons
and though I know nothing about you
there's a movement of feeling
spontaneous and strangely impersonal
which I think of as love.

I don't know why this happens
or what it means.
I think I'm learning that you are my species
my kin.
I think I'm learning
what it means to be human.

My daughter Davina will be 21 in a few days. I was wondering today if and when she'll become a mother and I a grandfather. Talking to You is primarily for *me;* however, I was thinking there might come a time when a grandchild of mine wonders about me. Reaches into the great Google "cloud" or whatever and reads some of my poems, maybe comes across: "An Old Man Talking to God" and spends an evening or two with these words. I would like that. I would like him or her to know a little about me. Not the curriculum vitae, not the personal details, but a modicum of insight into who I am, partly because some of who I am will be there in my grandchild's blood and being, just as my love of children seems to have passed on to Davina.

I would very much like Davina to love and marry a good man and that they will conceive and raise children of noble character who will be as lights in the world. And I pray that You will help them stay together just as you have helped us to stay together for twenty-six years.

I married in my late forties. It was, in a sense, an arranged marriage. You basically fused us together, even though we hardly knew one another and had no feeling of interest in or attraction to one another. There was no courtship, no romance, no falling in love, no excitement, no passion. It was as though You decided that we should be man and wife, and that was what happened. We really had no choice in the matter. We spent the first two years together in a kind of polar limbo, polar in the sense that we were so different, so opposite in every way that we couldn't even communicate with one another about basic issues like what should we have for dinner, and polar in the sense that we were frozen apart, stark in our separate spaces, both desperately unhappy but determined not to walk away, both of us having been married before and both too old and too despairing to go through all the messiness and pain of divorce and then go out and find someone else and start all over again. If it hadn't been for You we would never have married, and if it hadn't been for You we would not still be married, because somewhere in there beneath the terrible rows and the private despair there was and is a bond, a union that persisted and persists, which is the gift You gave us. It has taken me over a quarter of a century to understand – or partially understand – this gift, and as much time to learn to live up to it. To learn –to put it another way – how to love.

Love is both a noun and a verb. The noun version, I believe, is the state of falling or being in love. It's something that happens to us. It feels like a wonderful gift but I think it's more like a fever, a spell or an enchantment. It doesn't last. It may simply expire, like a fire in straw; it may (and often does) turn into its opposite; or it may evolve into something deeper and more stable, more mature. Love as a verb is conscious: "*I choose to love you, to go on loving you…*" a choice that is renewed over and over again regardless of what the other person has done, (unless it harms me), regardless of unfulfilled expectations or desires.

I know a couple in England whose marriage has been loving and peaceful from the very beginning. The wife told me she dreamt that she was walking around one of those globes with small mirrors all over its surface that revolve and send areas of light all over a dance floor; she was flicking a few grains of dust from its glossy surface with a feather duster. When she awoke she understood that this was an image or a symbol of their marriage. All it took was a little light routine maintenance. Ours, on the other hand, has been the kind of struggle Churchill used to make speeches about in the second world war.

It was an idea I once had that if we wanted marriage to work we would have to make sacrifices for it. So then marriage is a…what? An entity or reality, important in itself, separate from my needs and wants and your needs and wants. We get married; we make a promise, each one of us, a commitment to do all we can, individually and together, to make our marriage work. It's more than personal. So then we have to acknowledge and confront whatever it is that each one of us says or does that threatens the marriage and *deal with it*. The idea I had about marriage also included the notion that being married would involve dismantling the walls of my ego and letting someone else into my life as I never had done before, and that in truly loving one person I would come closer to loving humanity. Those, initially, were merely notions, things that others had told me or that I had read somewhere or that I knew with a kind of knowing that had not been earned or experienced. Now I've lived it through many hard years. I've learned how to love, how to consciously love.

The Coat

I came back one night from a walk

It was one of those nights
when you go out and it seems as if the world's gone crazy
this big mad wind roaring and blustering around
all over the place
Not really cold, just mad
Parked cars rocking
like glossy beasts stirring in their sleep
and bits of paper and leaves
skipping down the street
and suddenly joining together in a spinning dance
and the trees swaying and creaking
roaring like the sea
tossing their shadows about in the light of streetlamps
I came back all glowy and tingling
with this wide mad laughter inside me
I felt rinsed, I felt clean and light
as thought the wind had blown the dust out of me
scoured away all the folds and knots in my heart
I took my coat off and hung it in the hall
and there was your old black duffel coat next to it
and it suddenly seemed strange
that your coat was hanging there next to mine
on the hooks in the hall in our home

Such a strange and wonderful thing that we'd met
and fallen in love
and got married
as though our orbits had converged and fused
in the enormous universe of random events
And I thought of all the years you'd lived
before we met
growing up in your parents' home
experiencing cats and flowers and snow
having your first period
and wondering who you were
having friends I never knew
and lovers I never met
And all the changes you went through
all the memories inside you
I 'll never share
And here's your coat
here in this house you live in with me
all those years of not even knowing that I existed
and here you are in this house that is our home
all the things that are our things
and the kids that are our kids
that crawled out of your body
into our hearts
our kids sleeping in rooms in the house that is our
home
I stood there in the hall
nuzzling your coat
smelling your smells in its thick softness
and I started crying
in a way that was deeper than sadness or joy
I snuggled your coat against my face
and I knew it and felt it and said it:
I love you

My mother suffered from Lou Gehrig's, or motor neuron disease, for eight years. She was a good woman, God. As no doubt You know. A good woman and a warm loving mother. She was an indomitable spirit. She was always absolutely determined that she was going to defeat her disease and walk free. We used to visit her in her nursing home room on the Kentish coast of England. I remember Davina, who loved ballet as a child, wanted to dance for "Grams" so we arrived one day with the cassette of the Sugar Plum Fairy and Davina danced to it in her ballet outfit while my mother sat in her wheelchair supported by cushions. She was making a strange choked braying sound which was all that her increasingly immobilized body could do to express laughter and joy, she whose laughter, the sounds of it and the merriness of her ruddy smiling face, are part of my childhood like trees and bird-song and dogs.

One sunny day we took Grams out in her wheelchair for a walk by the sea. Down the gently sloping cliff path and along the walkway on top of the sea wall, quiet waves, gulls, kids flying kites, dogs on leads, smells of ice cream and drying seaweed. Then back up the sloping path, helped by a sturdy young stranger since Grams was heavy. We had tea and biscuits in an outdoor café and chocolate-covered ice cream for Davina. Grams was beam-smiling lopsidedly and sipping her tea through a straw. We sat around the table singing nursery rhymes.

*There was an old name man named Michael
Finnegan*
    He grew whiskers on his chinagan
    The wind came up and blew them in again
    Poor old Michael Finnegan begin again

And…

    Row row row the boat
    Gently down the stream
    Merrily merrily merrily merrily

Life is but a dream

One night, months later, I was sitting by her nursing-home bed, wind and rain at the window, the sound of her shallow breathing coming more and more slowly as though the sea had gone to sleep. I was holding her hands and praying to You. At some point I realized that she was still fighting… she was STILL FIGHTING. She was still determined that she was going to beat this thing, get out of bed and go for a walk by the sea, or bustle about cutting the toenails of old people who couldn't do it themselves, something she had done in her more active days and for which she was given a T-shirt with "Rose the Toes" on the front. I was awestruck by her tenacity, but I also knew it was her time to go. I leant over her and put my arms around her and murmured over and over again: *"You can let go no, mum. You can leave… they're waiting for you. …it's time to go mum… it's okay… let go now…"* and finally she left. She died.

Oh Rose…

They sailed in from some unknown country
landed unannounced on your quiet shores
went about their business efficiently
and with no clear expression of intent.
There was no reason given for their arrival
no old rekindled feud, no motive for revenge
or animosity. Anonymous and ruthless
they subjugated villages and towns
siphoned off your power
made desolate and numb
the country that they crossed.
By this time they were known for what they were
alarms and warnings sounded
counter-attacks were launched
defensive lines were drawn.
But forward, ever forward they advanced
unhurried and appalling in their progress.

You watched them take your country over
like a long dark shadow
that grew and deepened through the years
but, weakened though you were
surrender never was an option
your banner rose into the sky
and rode the sea-winds buoyant as a kite.
The circle tightened
sealed you inside your castle
made an exile of you
from your own beloved land.
Implacable, they infiltrated walls and gates
camped in courtyards
scanned the keep where, still defiant
you'd retired and launched their last assault on you.
Tired, sapped by years of battle
you fought on, your courage
gleaming in the sunlight like a golden shield.
At last the final door burst open
and there they were upon you
like a pack of silent wolves

But theirs was no victory
the only ground they gained
was ground you would have yielded
some time in the future.
The part that makes you who you are
the stubborn secret place
with all its treasures and its mysteries
remained inviolate
an undiscovered crystal
pool of dew within a rose.
When they smashed the door down
and destroyed the final refuge
you were no longer there;
their only prize a single silver hair
and laughter fading in the air

Maybe she was so stubborn in her resolve to reclaim her bodily strength that You were unable to guide and free her. It may be that if we, the members of my species, are for whatever reason closed off from You – like the man in the alley holding a container of acid – then You have no way of influencing or guiding us. Which is, I realize, to suggest that You are not, in fact, omnipotent. If You don't mind my saying so. I'm straying into the domain of spiritual speculation and paradox here, so I'll just offer this up to You then scoot off for some lunch:

If You were omnipotent then we would have no free will. You created the universe according to certain… what shall I call them?… certain principles or laws or dynamics. One of these laws, I believe, is that these laws be consistent. This makes sense to me even though as I ponder these matters I feel like a young chipmunk trying to gauge the size and history of Everest. These laws are an expression of Your will. I think You ceaselessly sustain and (maybe) strengthen them. Because You love us You gave us free will, which is one of the characteristics that render us human. Whether or not we seek to know and follow Your will, that's up to us.

I may have talked about this before. Never mind.

When my mother was lying there breathing once a minute and still fighting for her life I asked You to tell me what to do. Afterwards, when I looked back, it seemed that I was doing Your will in helping her to let go. It was as though You used me to pick her up and carry her away from her body into Your domain. Wherever that may be. In doing so you released her from an increasingly burdensome body, and, as a by-product, freed me from all fear of death. The woman who gave birth to me, the woman who carried me in her womb and then pushed me out into the world… I helped her die, certain (without knowing how or why) that there was somewhere else for her to go.

I've been remembering a little girl I met when I was teaching poetry writing in England. She was a sad little waif of a girl with red - rimmed eyes. We were writing poems in which something in nature speaks about itself. A boy wrote a poem about the wind that I liked so much I kept a copy:

I am the wind
I whisper to the whirling world
I am the wind
I whistle to the waves, the wonderful waves
I am the wind
I am the whispering wonderful wind

I have a secret
The secret that blows the breeze away
To an unknown land
I have a secret
That topples the tall trees like a terrible tornado
I have a secret
That nobody knows

The little girl was stuck so I borrowed her pencil, ask her questions, wrote down her answers then read it back to her. She smiled, wonderfully, when she heard it.

At the end of the workshop I gathered my books and materials and said goodbye. As I walked to the door the little girl came after me, took my hand and said, *"Can I come with you?"* It pierced my heart. I hugged her and said, *"No, I'm sorry."* I walked down the corridor or and out into the car-park and sat in my car for a while. She'll be in her 20s by now. I hope she's okay. Do You know the little girl I'm talking about? I don't recall her name . Everything is there in You. Nothing is lost or unknown. Please bless her life with love and happiness. Temperate, stable happiness… the best kind.

This morning I was running a poetry writing workshop with children of about the same age. Eight, nine years old. While they were reading riddles to one another I was looking through a book of poems written by one of the students. There was one about Hawaii, about why she liked it, and it ended with the line saying that it was the last place she was with her dad before he died…

I told her how much I liked her Hawaii poem and gave her a hug. I was about to tell her how sorry I was, but then I realized it wasn't right for me to do that… it wouldn't have helped her in any way, in fact it would probably have made her feel sad again. She knew that I knew and that was enough. There's a space in me which I think of as my inner. It's quieter and much deeper and wider than my heart. My heart reacts; my inner responds. I can see her at her desk drawing an imaginary creature. I offer her presence to You and ask You to heal her heart.

In my first year as a teacher, about 50 years ago, the parents of a 10-year-old boy in my class came to see me after school to tell me they were getting a divorce. They wanted me to know because they were concerned about their son, a quiet boy with brown eyes, dark hair, and a slow deliberate way of speaking. He was sitting outside the classroom as we spoke. Next day I asked him if he was okay… or rather, I started to, but he immediately recognized the concern in my voice and expression and said very clearly and firmly that he was fine, that he didn't want to talk about it. I nodded and moved on, let go of my sympathetic impulse, realizing that he needed the classroom to be a place that was familiar and stable, and that he needed space and freedom to heal. He liked to listen to stories on the listening center. Sitting on cushions over in the corner off the classroom with headphones on whenever he could. Later he wrote a story about a machine that would go roaring up and down the streets crashing houses and gardens and parked cars. Somehow the story ended with the machine being stopped and taken to its home, which was what it had been looking for.

I once met a couple named Mauricio and Rebecca Wild, who started a school in Ecuador. Rebecca wrote a book about it, and this book was the inspiration for the school I started in Arcata years later. In the grounds of their school there was a small cabin or hut where the children would gather. One day she heard terrible weeping coming from it. It was her son. When she looked inside the other children told her he was fine and that she should leave them alone. Which she did. Later she learned that her son was telling the story of how he burned his hand quite badly when he was a little boy, and in telling the story he was re-experiencing the pain in his hand and releasing it. All of this happened quite spontaneously. It was possible because she and Mauricio trusted children and gave them space and freedom to move around, to be attuned to their inner impulses and follow them. These impulses would uncover and heal psychic wounds through movement or expression of some kind, like the boy in London writing the machine story. After decades spent working with children and young people I have come to understand how important it is that we trust children and young people… that we teach them, or help them to learn, what they need to live as citizens, as members of their community, and that we love them unconditionally and are conscious always of what A.S. Neill called "The God in each child".

Sometimes gulls gather here where the creek flows along its channel in the sand before reaching the sea. They dip in their pale yellow beaks, each with its orange knob, and drink. They sit in the shallow flow and rinse their plumage. Sometimes the creek waters are several inches deep; today it's a shallow sparkling rivulet. Back there where it runs between rocks, small bubbles float on its rippling surface, and some of them remain there perched on the accelerating flow down the sandy slope. Even though it's shallow, the rippling water chafes at its sandy bank, sections of which intermittently collapse into the flow sending small waves across the creek and releasing hundreds of sand grains that roll along the creek bed glinting minutely in the sun.

There are minor events occurring all the time, wherever I look. Waves reaching their limits, rolling up the sandy gradient and rolling back to collide with the next wave as it advances, the encounter creating exploding regions of spray. A tiny dark bug is walking across this page. The quickly moving shadow of a pigeon has just crossed over me. Seawater is cascading over colonies of mussels that cling to the rock over there to my right. And the creek goes on sliding across the sand. I hear the softly tumbling sounds of running water and smell the wet brown smells of it.

It has scents and flavors, this cold clear water flowing past me into the sea. Scents and tastes of where it's been, of the soils and rocks, the roots and leaves, the tiny granules sucked from inland banks, frog cells and dust and pesticides, I'm thinking of salmon picking up the faintest traces of these smells and flavors to follow them back through the salty sea to their source, their home. Do You hold everything that has ever happened within your magnitude, God? All the minor events? Does the event of that soft white feather wind-skipping across smooth beige sand cease to exist as the feather drops into the creek and sails away into the foaming sea? It happened. The feather traveled on that part of its journey, and the fact that it did so is infinite. And so are all the other minor events occurring right now within the arc of this small bay. The feather will be slowly dismantled to become specks in the tide. Some of it may be drawn up into the sky, float inland, fall into a creek, flow seawards and be swallowed by a gull to become part of another feather, or of a webbed foot.

Skins

We have all been inside each other
lived within the skins of plums and rabbits.

Where did we bury our memory of stones?
What we call history
goes no deeper than a looking-glass.
What we call the world is what we need.

This is the edge we say, this is the self.

I want to tingle, and be still
so that in the silence
it will all come back to me

and I to it

All those memories in water, those molecular hints and whispers, memories of mint and pine cone, willow and deer piss.

The pool remembers everything the sea remembers.

This creek has a prehistoric lineage. Makes me think that perhaps there are no boundaries between past and present. My cells are constantly dying and being replaced, and this body will eventually rejoin the great Out-thereness of the material domain along with my ability to perceive through my senses, my digestive system and so on. My mother and father are buried in a Kentish hillside not far from the sea but there are traces or imprints of both of them in me, and of their parents and grandparents and great grandparents. I am flavored by my ancestors as this creek is flavored by its journey. How much of me is the man who was born Karl Rosenbaum on May 22, 1938 in London, and how much was already part of the blueprint set in place when I was conceived? How much of my story was is written by those who came before me? How much of my struggle is theirs? And here's another question, and I feel an answer of "Yes" even before I fully articulate it …

This blueprint I was born with – genetic traits, temperamental characteristics, astrological configuration maybe, all the pre-ordained, already in place stuff - is this

what we call "Fate"? Fate being the factors or forces that
influence us if we do not transcend them… But if we are
lucky or sufficiently blessed to evolve beyond the blueprint,
or to free our house of squatters, is this the more spacious
domain we call "Destiny"? This is the question to which I
sense the answer "Yes".

There are at least twenty meters of creek flowing
across the sand before it merges into the sea, and it's a
couple of meters wide over there. There's plenty of water,
plenty for everyone. Half a dozen gulls float in and land in
the creek for a communal bathe and drink. Sip flap preen
sip… everybody's happy. Then another gull, white chest,
gray wings, white tail, lands in the middle of the convivial
group and immediately goes on the offensive, flapping its
wings, thrusting its beaked head forward, even pecking quite
fiercely those gulls slow to move away. Soon it has the creek
to itself. The rest of the gulls have flown off round the
headland in search of a more peaceful spot.

I find myself disliking this dominant gull. I think of it
as a gangster commandeering a full Jacuzzi with a Clint
Eastwood snarl and a big gun. *"You're greedy and
arrogant,"* I tell it as it stands in solitary triumph, sipping at
the waters that dance around its skinny legs. I know that I'm
judging it from a human and therefore irrelevant perspective.
This, I remind myself, is what creatures do. It's how You
created them. We can make choices; they can't. You made
me a human being, but there's animal in me – survival
instincts, community, territoriality, sex... So I recognize the
scenario that just took place – the dominant gull driving
away all other gulls so that he has sole access to the plentiful
drinking and bathing waters of the creek. He spends a lot of
time trying to swallow a dead starfish but can't quite force his
beak wide open enough and gives up. Soon another gull
lands and it picks up the starfish in its beak. This infuriates
the dominant gull which goes into attack mode, flapping and
pecking and squawking. The other gull drops the starfish and
flies away. Dominant gull walks across the creek and along

the beach. He stands by the sea, looking out across the waves. He is at peace only because he is alone, and because his territory and its resources belong to him exclusively.

I believe Your world, the world You fashioned for us, holds an abundance of resources, enough for everyone. It would not be in Your nature to create a home for Your creatures that could not meet their needs, because You love us and do not wish us to suffer. I recognize the force that drives dominant gull all to stake his claim on the creek and deny all other gulls access to it, even though there's more than enough for a hundred gulls. I recognize it because it's in me.

I want it all to myself.
You can't have any.
This is mine!
If you don't go away I will hurt you.
Give it to me now!

A big difference between dominant gull and me is that I am a toolmaker. I have a clever brain. So if I'm playing the dominant gull role I have more than a beak at my disposal. As in…

I am sealing off the creek with an electric fence or a minefield.

I'm crouched on the bank in a concrete bunker, machine gun at the ready, and all you guys needing water, you can go and look somewhere else.
Or…

I pay a dominant gull lawyer lots of money for a document that states that I own the creek, and then I subdivide the creek into lots and sell them at very high prices to people who also have a dominant gull lawyers and dominant gull accountants and dominant gull financial experts and through a series of complicated and rather risky maneuvers dominant gull people in high buildings far from the creek are making enormous amounts of money which is unfortunate for those who live near the creek because they've lost their right of access to the creek and can't find water to drink or cook or keep themselves and their children clean and healthy.

It's only a matter of time before these gull people, the ones who have difficulty finding water, get so angry that they band together and make their way to the places where the high buildings are and they attack these buildings and confront the dominant gull financiers and lawyers and accountants and bankers and so forth and demand that they stop acquiring and holding so much to themselves and that they share with others according to principles that are fair and gull human.
As in…

Harmony is more important than money.
Let those who have much help those who have little.
Let the one who stands help the one who has fallen.
Let those who are clever help those who are not clever.
Let those who know where they are going guide those who are lost.
Let no man own so much that there is not enough for others.
Let us all strive to be human.

Not long after I arrived in Java, Unolv, a Norwegian friend who had lived there for years, took me on a trip to Bandung, and I remember that on the way we visited some of his Indonesian friends. We sat on a patio at the back of the house. Bamboo, banana plants... we drank sweet tea in cups with lids on them, and nibbled Indonesian cookies. They spoke reasonably good English and when we needed help Unolv translated. I remember thinking how *ordinary* the conversation was: *"Have you met the England queen?... Are you married?... Do you like Indonesia?..."*
Because these were the first Indonesians I'd really talked to I put aside my characteristic English snottiness (*"These people are not terribly interesting darling..."*) and talked about the topics they introduced openly and straightforwardly, smiling a lot and nodding. So we spent an hour or so together in this way, and then it was time to continue our journey, so we said goodbye. As we walked

away I had a curious experience… I felt what seemed to be fine elastic threads that were attached to my heart and that were stretching longer and longer as we walked towards the car, and as we drove away I felt these threads snapping and recoiling into my heart. It both saddened and puzzled me. I told Unolv about this and he said that when Indonesian people, especially the Javanese, meet someone for the first time they… how did he put it?… they seek to feel what this person is like inwardly. They seek to witness his or her nature. So when they are asking these apparently banal questions, introducing these very ordinary topics, they're listening to the tones in person's voice, gazing at their face, tasting (as it were) the whole person, the feeling of the person. If they like what they find, they open their hearts and a bond is formed. Apparently they liked what they sensed about me because they opened up to me. I wasn't trying to appear sophisticated, or intellectual, and I wasn't being patronizing as Westerners often are in "developing" countries. Within the rather uninteresting conversation bonds were being formed between me and each one of my hosts. Tea and empathy, one might call it. None of which I was aware off, until we were departing and the fine bonds stretched and broke with a series on loss pangs. Ow! Ohhh!

It's a very different way of being with one another, I realized. The Indonesians call Americans "Psychic tigers" because they're so direct, so straight from the shoulder, and, relatively speaking, forceful and aggressive. (Which is why I needed the bull dream.) Americans, in my experience, rarely make space in themselves into which they draw or usher the person they're talking to. There's a lot of head, or mind, and there's a lot of noisy, reactive feeling – heart rather than inner feeling. What Indonesians gain from their culture is a feeling of close-knit community, a quality I believe You wish for all of us. But what they lack is a strong sense of themselves as individuals with the capacity to innovate, to change the world. This is also a quality I believe You wish for all of us. Maybe what the world needs is a new kind of human being, one who incorporates the characteristics of both ways of living. Someone who blends the bonding traits, the "we" ness of the Javanese with the self-assertiveness, the "I" ness, of Americans. In a sense this might be termed as a fusion of the heart (Indonesia) and mind (American), with the proviso that heart in this context means: "inner feeling" or, to use an Indonesian word, *"jiwa"*.

This desired blend of national characteristics is, when I step back to consider it, a kind of dream, an idea born in my mind and likely to go no further. Except that people do change. My bull dream implanted in my being the force of Americanness.   There I was feeling completely overwhelmed by what I was experiencing as the crassness of my new American acquaintances, drawing fastidiously into my inner sanctum like an English aristocrat crouched in his castle keep as barbarians defecate on his cherished lawns and steal his cattle. We can be added to. We can change.

However, the notion that we'd all acquire deeper, wider, more global inners if we were able to live in other countries, while attractive and worthy, is not likely to be realized. Even if it were to happen, and I suppose there are a lot more of us flying off to live in other countries than there were forty years ago, there is no guarantee that we will be open to the energies of our new country of abode. At least some of the terrorists who flew into the World Trade Center had lived in America for a while without learning to love it. I remember how the expatriate community in Java's capital city Jakarta lived in a kind of Euro–American bubble, so much so that an architect friend who was designing additional buildings for the primarily American international school proposed – with his tongue in his cheek -to erect a statue on the campus with the legend: *"This is an Indonesian"* inscribed on its base.

My childhood was so darkened by an enormous war that I've lived since then with the urgent hope that things would get better. That we would be so haunted by the death and destruction we had unleashed that our traumatized inners would gather on some bloodstained plain strewn with smoldering shrapnel and corpses, thick with the stench of smoke from burning cities and horror chimneys and we would all bow our heads and join hands and weep at the horror of what we had done. And we would all cry, "*Never again!*" We would look into one another's eyes, eyes once filled with hatred or fear, but that now burn with a desperate desire to love and to start all over again…

… and I doubt that there's been a single hour since then in which a human being was not killing another human being.

I know that a light and happy heart is more open to your Guidance. At this moment, I really do not know if the darkness I am seeing is mine or if it is objectively real. Maybe this is a false dichotomy. Darkness exists. It's out there and it's in me. I'm not depressed, or bipolar, or ill. I spent time this morning with children and my heart is still smiling. They are at one end of their lives and I'm at the other end. My closet is full of the past: their closets are full of the future.

So how are you planning to save the world, Emmanuel?

If young people, with their strength and idealism, were to move together in an irresistible global revolution and take over…

if we or at least most of us, could live in at least one other country for at least two years….

if we, lots of us, could re-enter the innocent domain of childhood as I did this morning, and make cleaning up our planet top priority so that our children's futures are not mired by our greed…

It doesn't work like this other, does it God? These are ideas. There may be truth in them, as there is in many of the ideas we formulate as we move towards collective crisis. My friend in Australia believes that ideas can change the world. I wish I could believe this, but I don't. If my mind is full of noise then no new idea, no matter how truthful, will get the attention it needs if it is to be understood. But to the extent that we are open to Your guidance, to that extent You move us into a better future.

I keep returning to this. We must love You or we die.

What a spindle spangle of a day! Look at all that
solar sparkle on the sea! The twinkle–flashiness of Allah…

Light

Watch the boat out there groove glitter
black, shrunk by distance, its
bright wake rolls of foil
widening across the glint.
Beyond it dimpled silver dims
to soft blue-gray haze
muffling horizons and remembered islands.

Watch the wave down there as it
curls over on itself
see how sunlight flares
within the rolling tunnel
lasering the jade concave.
See how dazzle dances over
foam and spray, reignites
the next green glossy hollow
spreads points and blades of liquid light
across the roaring tilt; a fractal mylar fizz
that bathes the brain in
incandescent shimmerings so brief
they cannot be looked at
only glimpsed.

The black boat butts the blue-green swell
tows gulls towards the harbor.

Whatever it may be out there
that moves us
its counterpart is already here within.
Why, then, this wonder? Is there a place
where beings live

There was a day my father was off at the pub quaffing his pints, his staccato laughter no doubt ringing throughout the bar and out into the street. By that time his fingers were stiff with arthritis and he was suffering from shingles. I was in his little yellow house cleaning his kitchen. The stovetop and oven were crusted with grimy scaly stuff from weeks of slightly inaccurate cooking, and as I scraped and scoured I found myself slipping into resentful mode: *"The old fart's drinking himself silly again while I'm here cleaning his sh…"* etc. All the years, the decades, of anger at my father's drinking, at seeing a cultured, funny, perceptive man turning into a remote bumbling sot… all this was alive in me, and I put down the scouring pad and the sponge and sat on the kitchen floor feeling anger and loss. At the same time I knew he wasn't going to be around much longer, and I saw how far apart we still were and that we had to work at finding ways back to one another before he died. I asked You to show me how I should feel towards him. I did my best to disengage from the anger and resentment and waited.

"It is right that you honor your father, and that you love him."

Oh… yes… well… thank you.

It wasn't easy. I wasn't sure what it meant, to "honor" someone, so I kept asking to feel it. I didn't want a dictionary definition, I wanted the quality alive inside me. Whenever I visited him, and whenever I remembered, I would ask You to help me honor him.

We'd listen to music together. Read poetry. We often sat at a bench outside his local pub enjoying the sunshine, the sparkling sea-clean air… I talked about my travels, about

Indonesia and Los Angeles, about Subud, about my writing.
We talked of God, and books. We were not yet close, but we
were comfortable.

Christmas came. He got so drunk they had to carry him
home from the pub and place him in his old armchair. We
went to see him. He was raving away about Jesus Christ and
Lady Julian of Norwich. He caught pneumonia. Hospitalized.
Double pneumonia. Nearly died.

I talked to my brother and sister about his drinking, and
wrote him a letter, which was from us, not just me. I said we
all loved him but that it was hard to show this, hard to be
with him when he was drunk because he was so distant and
sarcastic. So we asked him to please stop drinking.
I sat by his hospital bed while he read. I'd never stood
up to him before, not like this. I could hear his chest
wheezing as he breathed. I didn't know how he was going to
react. Maybe with anger. Maybe he'd tell me he never
wanted to see me again. I was asking You to help us.
He put the letter down, turned to me, smiled, and said:
*"Well as a matter of fact I came to the same conclusion
myself yesterday."*

He didn't stop completely. I don't think any of us
expected that. But he cut way back. We became good
friends, he and I. And it was safe to visit him with Davina.

The Old King
We have come to pay our respects
to the old king
in his little white palace
close to the sea
where roses bloom in yellow praise
walls remember candlelight and saints.

Today the old king
sits thin and frail on his throne.
His voice speaks from a heart so hushed

that words surrender to the silence they arise from.
You study his stiffening knuckles
his tentative step
with a child's dispassionate gaze.
You draw him a picture
of sunlight and rain
and the house where you live
as queen of the summer leaves
and the palace is filled with your rippling talk
the innocent light in your hair.
You reach for the world
the old king is slowly relinquishing
as his life draws into itself
like a symphony rinsed to its primal theme.

If he were here, down on the shoreline
he'd crouch in the breakwater lee
watching you wonder at details
wet stones brown as chestnuts
strands of net and kelp
damp limb of a dismantled dollie.
Then he'd lift his gaze
to contemplate the long horizon
where distant sea-birds ride the wind
and disappear.

I didn't know that it mattered so much, how things were
between my parents and me. I didn't realize that whatever
issues there were between us must be resolved before they
died. Looking back I think You were guiding us so that we
left Los Angeles, Amelia and Davina and I, and came to live
in a cottage on a beautiful English manorial estate a few
miles from my parents' home. Through me I believe You
helped my mother die, then You brought my father and me
closer to one another than I would ever have thought
possible, so that when he died there was no residue of
bitterness, just regret at the loss of a good friend. I have a
strong feeling that if our parents die before we have

reconciled any issues we have with them, if they die before we have forgiven one another and learnt to love one another as best we can, then we, the survivors, are left with pain in our hearts that is hard to release. And I believe that mothers and fathers who die without knowing that their children love them… I think it's harder for them to go on. I believe this to be a truth.

But it's never too late. Even years after their deaths, it's not too late to forgive them, to ask their forgiveness, to tell them that we love them. So that they can go on. So that they can rise more freely and lightly towards You.

Talking to You has become a habit. Not as an autopilot routine but as a regular feature of my consciousness. It's close to being an integral part of my default mode, which was the wish and prayer I felt a while ago. Sometimes the talking to You is verbal. Sometimes it's… well, it's not verbal, not articulated. It's actively felt.
Talking to You has changed me in at least two ways:
One. Most of the time, unlike before, I'm quietly, temperately happy. And if I'm not, if I'm in grouchy–old–man–with–a–somewhat–dodgy–body mode, then I recognize this much more quickly than before and, inspired by the irrefutable proposition that it's better to feel okay than not okay, ask You to free me of negative stuff and make my heart happy. The ratio of this working as opposed to not working is progressively improving.
Two. My heart is more loving. The human beings whose paths cross mine each day, whoever they are, whatever the context… I love them. I don't necessarily feel moved to give them warm hugs, or to express this love in any way. As this feeling moves in me, moves in my guts, I am glad that each of my species I meet is here, is alive. Yes. Please bless this person Allah.

Blurry waking up… bedside clock says 4.17. I'm lying in the limbo between wakefulness and sleep, unable to enter the one or return to the other. A cozy tugging of blankets round shoulders and chin. How strange, this state of sleep, this country I left for no clear reason and that I'm unable to go back to. I sense the aftershock of a bad dream that I don't remember.
Please God may I feel Your peace may I feel Your love.

Everything is so quiet. An early car on a nearby road. An owl hoo hoo hoos softly in the eucalyptus grove a few houses away. I reach out through the cold air and open the curtain. Strong moonlight out there. Silvery, enchanted. I lie in bed for a long time watching trees in the garden moving gently in the soft wind, arrangements and rearrangements of light and dark. The full moon is hidden by trees, as are the stars. I'm thinking of silvery ripplings on the sea's surface…
Yes! Go!

I'm driving down an empty Highway One. Round Devil's Slide, a few miles south… then turn right and park near Moss Beach Woods. Down the steps to the beach. Here we are. Shoes and socks off. Brrr! Cold January sand. Look at the big fat silvery – golden moon up there, and a long palisade of rounded clouds above the horizon, silvery and

plump like irradiated pillows… and oh my goodness see the light on waves, the quiet waves, more lovely than I'd imagined, ripplings and sinuous ridges of liquid dark-toned gold-molten dancings of moonlight, clair de lune. I'm standing in numbingly cold wavelets and there are ripples of reflected light stroking my body, and I'm thinking of our cat, of stroking the silky fur on his back and feeling him purr purr purr…
An early heron, a dark gaunt shape, flies above the waves, crying its harsh "cronk".

Too slowly to be discerned, the sky is turning lighter and lighter. Silvery pearly pinkish, an early blushing. The moon is a disc of pale apricot sinking into a pinky-gray cloud.

Vertical multitasking. Dry my feet on my hoodie, socks and boots back on. God be here within me and all around me…

I'm lying on cold sand looking at the enormous distant sky, a dome of pale light soft as mist and clear as rock-pools, feeling the slow swing from night to day, old man on the sea's crinkly edge holding my hands towards the sky, singing a wandery song, arthritic column of temperate happiness, feeling the planet turn and the cold dawn wind on my face.

Someone once told me that we have to die over and over again. The fetus dies to become baby dies to become toddler dies to become child dies to become youth dies to become adult dies to become elder… Is this all the dying we can do before our heart stops? No. I want… what is it?… to be dying continuously. I want the me I am now, the me I was last week and yesterday and here, now, this early morning, this familiar present me… I want this me to die, to turn into a me who is closer to You. Always I want this, even when I don't remember that it is this that I want. This familiar me, may this me die today and become a me who is closer and closer and closer to You.
That's all. There's nothing else.